"The powerful story of a remarkable man and a town whose love is nothing short of inspirational!"
—**Dr. Allen Hunt**, Senior Advisor, Dynamic Catholic

"After reading about *The Most Amazing Harvest* I knew this would be a beautiful story of an incredible life. Carl will be an inspiration to many."
—**Jon Gordon**, Best Selling Author of
The Energy Bus and *The Carpenter*

"A beautiful story about the human spirit that touches the heart and reminds us all that we are not alone."
—**Patty Ricard**, Dental Coach, Clinical Mastery Lab

"A touching story that will make you laugh, cry, and more importantly think about living life to the fullest with your family, friends, community, and God! A true inspiration from a man and his guardian angel on how precious life truly is."
—**Amy Schneider**, Friend in Dentistry

"What an encouraging story about love, service, community, and a life lived to the fullest—what more could one hope for!?"
—**Cari Nelson**, LPC, NCC, Licensed Professional
Counselor, and life-long friend

The Most Amazing Harvest

The Most
AMAZING
HARVEST
THE MAN BEHIND THE STORY

*The continued love story of how a town
came together for one of their own*

PAM BATES
PAULA PATTY

NEW YORK

LONDON • NASHVILLE • MELBOURNE • VANCOUVER

THE MOST AMAZING HARVEST
THE MAN BEHIND THE STORY

Published in New York, New York, by Morgan James Publishing. Morgan James is a trademark of Morgan James, LLC. www.MorganJamesPublishing.com

Scripture texts in this work are taken from the *New American Bible, revised edition* © 2010, 1991, 1986, 1970 Confraternity of Christian Doctrine, Washington, D.C. and are used by permission of the copyright owner. All Rights Reserved. No part of the New American Bible may be reproduced in any form without permission in writing from the copyright owner.

Excerpts from the English translation of the Catechism of the Catholic Church for use in the United States of America Copyright © 1994, United States Catholic Conference, Inc. -- Libreria Editrice Vaticana. Used with Permission. English translation of the Catechism of the Catholic Church: Modifications from the Editio Typica copyright © 1997, United States Conference of Catholic Bishops—Libreria Editrice Vaticana."

Mercyme Music (ASCAP) / Wet As A Fish Music (Co-Pub) (ASCAP) / (admin at Essentia MusicPublishing.com [3]). All rights reserved. Used by permission.

ISBN 9781642799347 paperback
ISBN 9781642799354 eBook
Library of Congress Control Number: 2019956181

Cover Design by:
Christopher Kirk
www.GFSstudio.com

Interior Design by:
Chris Treccani
www.3dogcreative.net

Morgan James is a proud partner of Habitat for Humanity Peninsula and Greater Williamsburg. Partners in building since 2006.

Get involved today! Visit
MorganJamesPublishing.com/giving-back

To our family, friends, and farmers for sharing
in this love story.

A special dedication to the memory of:
Steve King—a great friend and Harvest farmer;
And Father Bruce Lopez—an integral part of
Carl's faith journey.

TABLE OF CONTENTS

FOREWORD

We met Pam and Paula on a cold December afternoon at the OSF HealthCare Children's Hospital of Illinois. We loved them immediately. They are real people, the kind you instantly bond with. Two things struck us, first, their faith is amazing and second, they have this glow about them that lights up a room. They embrace Matthew 5:16, "*In the same way, let your light shine before men, that they may see your good deeds and praise your Father in heaven.*"

We were brought together that day by our shared desire to help children and families as they battle pediatric cancer. Carl Bates had pediatric cancer. But it didn't define him. He counted his blessings and lived life to the fullest.

Their mission in writing *The Most Amazing Harvest* is the same mission we embrace at OSF Children's Hospital with our Heller Center for Kids with Cancer, you are never alone, and have trust in your faith with God.

Pam and Paula have written a beautiful love story, framed in faith, family, friendship and community. This story and Carl Bates the man, speak to the mantra that surviving the battle against pediatric cancer is just the start. The world needs to witness the humility and decency lived in Carl Bates' faith journey.

You will love his antics, his courage and his journey of faith.

Our wish together is that each child facing cancer has the chance and ability to live their life to the fullest, just like Carl.

Annette and John Heller
Founders of The Heller Center for Kids with Cancer at OSF Children's Hospital of Illinois

PREFACE

"The harvest is abundant, but the laborers are few;
so ask the master of the harvest to send out laborers
for her harvest."
(Luke 10:2)

"The Most Amazing Harvest" was a bit of a phenomenon for a while, on Facebook, on television, in magazines, newspapers, and websites. It was spread across the world. This feel-good story went viral. The local television station set this in motion when they came to the farm and told the story and shared the harvest picture. National news stations picked it up. Then other worldwide stations saw it and reported as well. It all started when a few farmers recognized that their friend was going to be struggling to get his harvest done. He had been diagnosed with metastatic cancer on July 31, 2015, and was in hospice care. This friend, Carl Bates, was a guy everyone could count on. It was said in one article that "he had his heart in the right place," and so when word got out that some farmers were going to help with his harvest, many more wanted to help. The plan was set and the day was chosen: September 25, 2015. There were ten combines, twelve grain carts, sixteen semi-trucks, and over forty farmers and helpers who kept everything running smoothly. And it was all donated.

Some generous Galva businesses also donated food and drinks for the farmers. Many women made lunch, dinner, and snacks for the day. Tables at the home farm were set up in the yard with the lunch consisting of BBQs, Subway sandwiches, chips, and all kinds of cookies and treats. As they prepared to move to the next field, they all stopped and grabbed their lunch and then were sent out with a donated mini cooler with drinks and snacks for their afternoon. A drone took an amazing picture of the combines all lined up and the day was a success. All 450 acres were harvested and taken to market within ten hours. This was made possible when the grain elevator, Rumbold & Kuhn, dubbed this day Carl Bates Day. They only accepted Carl's loads during those ten hours.

So, who was this man that inspired The Most Amazing Harvest? What is the rest of his story? What are the moments that molded the life of this soul while he was here on earth?

Carl was placed in a particular time and a specific place with people for him to love and with people who would love him. There is no such thing as a coincidence; this is a God-incidence. Carl encountered God through his experiences. Some good, some sad, some we just don't understand. As his knowledge and faith grew, his soul was prepared for its purpose. This purpose was to love God and His people here on earth and spend eternity with Him in Heaven.

ACKNOWLEDGMENTS

The farmers–you demonstrated how to love your neighbor.

Our families and friends–your support and encourage-ment gave us the confidence to keep going. We are blessed to have you as part of our story. A special thank-you to Lou Patty.

Contributors–for your willingness to share your time, talent, and treasure. Dr. Allen Hunt, Jon Gordon, Patty Ricard, Amy Schneider, Cari Nelson, Annette Hartman, Joy Hernandez-But-ler, Wendy Fitzgerald, Emily Bailey, Deacon John Holevoet, Ava and Griffin DeWolfe, Scott Mitchell, Denise Fishel, Roger Luft, Michelle Mersman and Ann VanWassenhove.

Helpers in the process–your guidance and suggestions were immeasurable. Bud McKirgan, Ryan Sumner, Heather Sellers, Kelly VanWinkle.

Our editing and publishing team–your belief in this story was humbling. Kevin Anderson for finding us a publisher. Brunella Costagliola, your editing expertise and kind comments were blessings. Janice Brown, thank you for your final proofreading and encouraging words. David Hancock, Bonnie Rauch and Morgan James Publishing teams for making it all happen.

INTRODUCTION

This is the story of a wonderful man, narrated by his guardian angel. Carl Bates was a farmer, a survivor, and we believe a saint.

Writing Carl's story was a labor of love. We were inspired by God to "tell his story!" That message was heard over and over the first year after his death. God wouldn't give up, so on the first anniversary of his death we took our initial book-writing trip to Galena, Illinois. Over the next three years we also took trips to Wisconsin, Tennessee, Iowa, Alabama, and Rome. These trips were always filled with holy moments, laughter, and tears.

Sharing the stories was a healing process, and we believe a true love story never ends. Carl wrote in a card once "Keep up the good work." We hope that by telling the simple story of an amazing, miraculous, peaceful life we are doing just that.

We want to help you realize the blessings and miracles in your life and we pray that you don't take them for granted.

May you enjoy getting to know this humble man and the Galva community that we call home.

God created us all to have life and live it to the fullest.

God Bless!

Pam and Paula

CHAPTER 1

Augustine aka "Gus"

*"Beside each believer stands an angel as protector
and shepherd leading him to life."*
CCC336 St. Basil

I have been with Carl since the beginning, the very beginning, and I love Carl. I'm pretty sure you will, too, as we unfold this journey. It was my job to share God's love with Carl, and it has been my honor and pleasure. You see, I am Carl's guardian angel. My name is Augustine but you can call me Gus.

When a child is born, a guardian angel is assigned to that child. According to scripture, Psalm 91:11-12, "For God commands the angels to guard you in all your ways. With their hands they shall support you, lest you strike your foot against a stone."

All angels are messengers from God, so we communicate God's love to our assignees in a million different ways. As a guardian angel, God has also given us the important task to keep them safe from harm, when possible, and to guide them through whatever trials may befall them. We pray with them and for them. Bringing them to their Heavenly home is our ultimate goal.

This story began when I got my assignment. It is quite a big deal; all of the Heavenly hosts are present for the announcements! The trumpets sound and there is singing and rejoicing. I was so excited when my name was called, I just knew I was going on an amazing adventure and I couldn't wait. I had been assigned to a baby boy, conceived in love. His family lived on a farm in central Illinois.

Galva, Illinois, would be my new home, population somewhere around three thousand. It is in the middle of the state and some would say it's the middle of nowhere. Corn and soybean fields surround the town. Barns full of cattle and hogs, and tall silos full of corn create the landscape. The folks who live there think they are pretty lucky to live a small-town life with larger metropolitan cities just forty-five minutes to the north and to the south.

Galva has been the home of many manufacturing businesses and it still blows a whistle at 7 a.m., noon, 1 p.m., and 5 p.m. These are a reminder of days gone past with the workday time clock. When the 5 p.m. whistle blows, the children in town know it is time to go home for dinner.

The downtown is full of mom-and-pop grocery stores, hardware stores, a drugstore, two women's clothing stores, a men's clothing store, a shoe store, and a Ben Franklin department store. They are all locally owned and operated.

There is a bakery in town that has a box under the counter where you put the money for the items you are taking—if you don't have the right change, you can put it in the next time. The people who live in Galva are trusting and honest. Their most popular item is their Swedish rusk—a hard sweet bread to dunk in coffee. Swedish rye bread is another favorite. Galva is near Bishop Hill, a settlement for many Swedish immigrants. The Swedish heritage is kept alive in this quaint colonial village. Galva also has Swedish roots and influences. The town is named after its sister city, Gavle, Sweden.

Galva has a theatre, with a candy shop next door. The candy shop is famous for their cinnamon rolls that they heat on the grill with lots of butter. Of course all the bins of candy are every child's dream. Kids always have something to do on Saturday afternoons and evenings. The booths are always full of teenagers and families.

The Galva Bowling Alley is another hot spot with eight lanes. They serve the best Sophie burger in town. This is a hamburger with grilled onions. Saturday mornings are when many children bowl in league and weeknights are the grown-up leagues. Saturday nights are open bowling.

They have an event every year in Galva called Sidewalk Days, when all the stores bring things out onto the sidewalk and mark their prices way down. The *Galva News* fills boxes with all the pictures they have taken throughout the year, and people stand for hours looking for pictures of people they know. There are games for the kids, including a greased pig contest. A local farmer donates one of his pigs and a fence is set up in the middle of the park. The pig is covered with shortening and then the children have to try and catch the pig, which is hard to hold. If they hold it down for thirty seconds they win a prize! They also have a penny scramble, where pennies are thrown in hay for the kids to find. Everyone gets to keep the money they find. This usually means their next stop is the candy shop for some penny candy.

The city built a Park District where they have ball diamonds that are busy all summer with tee ball, Little League, softball, and adult leagues. The swimming pool with a shallow end for smaller children, a deep end with two diving boards, and an Olympic-size area with lanes painted on the floor was one of the first in the county. Two tennis courts, a basketball court, and a Putt-Putt golf course give families a place to play together.

Other parks in Galva include Veterans Park in the middle of the square downtown, with a fountain you can throw pennies in and make a wish. Wiley Park is across from the elementary school and has an ice skating rink every winter. Mr. Rodgers, a Galva science teacher who lives across from the park, made a homemade Zamboni to keep the ice in good shape for skating. He also keeps extra skates on his porch for those who need to borrow a pair. Washington Park on the south side of town has a picnic pavilion that is always in use for family reunions.

It is a beautiful town, full of hardworking people with big hearts, ready to lend a hand or share a meal. It has a nickname: The City of Go. And that fits. Galvans show up, they go out, they make a difference without counting the cost.

The virtues and values the residents portray were learned in the many churches in this small town: Baptist, Christian, First Methodist, Grace Methodist, Lutheran, Congregational, Assembly of God, and St. John's Roman Catholic. These buildings were all filled with people seeking God's will in their lives.

Things changed over my time in Galva; businesses came and went, schools were torn down and new ones were built, a stoplight was considered once but it never happened. The people, however, didn't change. They have always been good people.

When I first met Carl, I loved to hover overhead while his parents were rocking him to sleep. He would smile and coo at me. From the beginning, he had a little mischievous look in his eye when he was smiling. His mom and dad always wondered what was so interesting up above their heads—it was just me. He didn't know why I was there, watching over him, but he wasn't afraid. We had a connection.

I loved the farm, the smell of the fresh hay in the barn, even the smells of the animals because it was so much a part of this family's culture. I loved the miracle of the seasons and the trust involved in the planting and knowing there would be a harvest. The beauty of all of God's creation was everywhere. The hard work that goes into each day was inspiring. If you didn't come home with sweat dripping off of you then you hadn't accomplished much. I loved Carl's family, the way they looked out for each other and got through everything together. I loved the adventures Carl and I experienced together.

Carl and I went through some good times and we encountered some challenges. This rambunctious little boy had a deep trust in our loving God. He didn't always recognize that his trust was in God, but you will hear how that was revealed through miracles and the trials he was given. My experience with Carl was a balance between "living life in the fast lane" and "slow and steady wins the race."

Through it all I tried to help Carl see that trials are allowed sometimes to get our attention. God wants us to stay close to Him. God never moves but sometimes we do. When things are going along fine, we sometimes forget about God. I also wanted Carl to know that God was walking beside him through it all, and that's where hope and peace, courage and strength come from. Carl never complained, he never worried, and was always at peace. He didn't always know where that came from, but I did!

We guardian angels aren't always recognized. Either people don't know about us or don't think about us much. In the end, Carl was very aware of me. He recognized times that I had helped avert danger and had asked God to grant him miracles. But most importantly, he knew God's love.

Life is a series of stories. Our experiences, our joys, our sorrows, how we loved, and how we were loved tells who we are.

The greatest story ever told is the story of salvation, and that story tells us that life does not end when we leave this world. God sent His son, Jesus, to die for our sins and to open the gates of Heaven for everyone. Eternal life is the goal, being the best version of ourselves while we are here, so we can be saints. I led him ultimately to his Heavenly home as a saint. And just so you know, saint Carl is praying for all of you!

You will notice, I called Carl "saint" with a lowercase *s*. I should explain a little about sainthood. Everyone who makes it to Heaven is a saint, not an angel as some may think. Angels are created different from humans. Sainthood is attainable for everyone. Doing great things is not necessary, just living a simple life with great love for God and His people. Receiving God's mercy and being merciful is how it is done. Sainthood with a capital S is when the Catholic Church investigates and attributes miracles through a process to call a person a canonized Saint.

I am going to tell you Carl's story. I will break it up into chapters; some will be long, and some will be short. Let's start with Carl's family.

CHAPTER 2

Family

"Train a boy in the way he should go; even when he is old,
he will not swerve from it."
(Proverbs 22:6)

Carl's dad, Edward Bates, grew up just a few miles from their home farm in Galva with two brothers and five sisters. His parents were Carl and Verla Bates. Ed was a Korean War veteran—something he barely ever mentioned because he saw things there that he just couldn't speak about. Ed's guardian angel, Bud, helped him to put those hard memories behind him. Bud helped Ed see that war experiences do not define us, even though it is gallant to protect our country. We can replace those bad memories with good ones and focus our life on the positive. I loved that in later years Ed would get together with his war buddies and their wives for weekend gatherings—they turned their bond into something fun and frivolous, not serious and heartbreaking.

When he returned home from the war, farming and 4H were very important to Ed. I learned all about 4H, which is a youth development organization found in most Midwest communities. It was inspiring to see young people learn life skills through completing projects in areas of their interest. That summer he went to a 4H camp for young adult leaders, White Eagle 4H camp. Being a 4H leader was always a blessing to Ed and to the members of his groups. He served as a leader for many years, teaching the 4H pledge and living it: "I pledge . . . my Head to clearer thinking, my Heart to greater loyalty, my Hands to larger service, and my Health to better living. For my club, my community, my country, and my world."

Carl's mom, Carol, grew up in Durand, Illinois, about three hours north of Galva. Her parents were Ernest and Margaret Mowers and she had three sisters. She and her sisters worked hard on the farm—they had thirty-two cows to be milked morning and night. She was active in 4H also. Carol and her sisters would hurry to get their chores done so they could go to Theodore's Barn Dance on the weekends, near Freeport. These girls did all kinds of dancing, but they especially liked square dancing and the jitterbug. Carol always had a good time. She was never going to be accused of being a wallflower! She kept her guardian angel, Michael, busy when they took the neighbor's Jeep joyriding in the fields.

Carol and Ed met in the summer of 1954 at White Eagle 4H leaders camp. Ed's current girlfriend had come to camp with him, but once Ed met Carol he let his girlfriend go home early. This is when Carol and Ed's relationship began. God had brought them together and they both had the same goal:

raise a loving family on a farm. Carol and Ed dated for about a year and a half, and they were married on October 28, 1956. Ed began farming with his brother Earl.

Carol and Ed loved to go square dancing and had matching square dance outfits—Carol with her full skirt and petticoat, and Ed with his matching western shirt and string tie. They would hurry off every Saturday night to promenade and do-si-do. Bud and Michael, their guardian angels, told me great stories of their young love and commitment to each other and their family.

Then came the day I knew it was a special day. God had let me watch Carol as I prepared for my assignment. It was hectic. Carol had canned forty-two quarts of beans and made several gallons of ice cream for the 4H ice-cream social. She was just getting ready to take a break and relax, when Carl decided to make his appearance.

Carol was excited that Ed had his first son. He was 9 lbs. 9 oz. and full of spunk! Carl Edward Bates was born July 14, 1960, in Kewanee, Illinois, after eighteen hours of labor—and that's when my duties began.

Carl was named after his grandfather, Carl Jennings Bates, and his father, Edward.

When Carl was born he had two older sisters—one was in Heaven, and her name was Carrie. She died during her birth due to the umbilical cord being wrapped around her neck. She loved to pray for her family; that was her mission and she did it well. Carrie's prayers helped me out now and then.

I've always felt it is unfortunate that people who lose children at an early age don't realize that God created them as a prayer warrior for their family. Carrie had a purpose and she will welcome her family when they join her in Heaven. Before I got my assignment it was one of my favorite things to do, watch families meet their children, siblings, or parents for the first time. All saints in Heaven appear to be the same age, right around their twenties. When children meet their parents, they see them as young people, and when parents see their children who have left earth at an early age, they see them grown up. There is so much joy in those moments of recognition and awareness of the goodness of God. The lame walk, the deaf can hear, and there is no pain or suffering. I'm tearing up just thinking about that joy!

His sister here on earth was Judy, and she was born on August 4, 1959, so just eleven months older. Even though Judy was older than Carl, he was the leader and would oftentimes get her in trouble with his dangerous ideas. Judy was Carl's sidekick. She was a lot like her mom in wanting to be helpful and sacrificing for others.

Carl's brother Ernie came along on February 23, 1962, when Carl was eighteen months old. He was the good kid, always following the rules and doing what he was supposed to. Watching the dynamics of the family, I always saw Carl as the prodigal son and Ernie as the good son who never caused much trouble. Ernie was very bright and got along with everyone. His humor was contagious, and he loved to have a good time.

Verla was born July 15, 1963, just the day after Carl turned three years old. Carl was her hero; she would do anything and everything he told her to. She loved to help Carl with the pigs.

He loved to antagonize her. He blamed a lot of things on Verla when they were growing up, and she would gladly take the blame. She always forgave him. Verla was the tomboy who loved to play softball and basketball. I'll never forget the time she won the greased pig contest at Sidewalk Days. It was so fun to watch but she sure was a mess when it was over.

With four young children it was a houseful—you might say, a little crazy. The other guardian angels and I had a great time. They wanted me to keep Carl from instigating so much trouble, but he had a spirit that couldn't be suppressed.

Carl and Judy had a bond that started early on. One of their favorite activities was sneaking out when mom was napping. He and Judy had a secret code at naptime—the little ones were still too young to join the fun. When mom—who really needed the nap—would fall asleep either in the girls' room or the boys' room, Judy or Carl would signal on the wall with a long scrape, the other would tap back short short, which meant the coast was clear and everyone was asleep. Then the adventure would begin. These two would stock up with Pepsi and Oreos and head outside. They liked climbing the silo or walking the rafters in the barn. Other times they would shimmy up the big tree in the front yard and count the cars going by.

It seemed to never occur to them that Mom was going to wake up and find them. Sometimes when danger seemed to be evident, I was the one waking her up. There was one time that the two of them were sixty feet up on the silo. When Carol found them, she took a deep breath and calmly told them she was going to town and would they like to go. Whew, never a dull moment!

Carol was always trying to be helpful on the farm. Ed and Carl were busy in the field, so she volunteered to take the baby calf to the sale barn. Well, the truck wouldn't start so she loaded the calf in the backseat of her car and away she went. This made me laugh but was also proof that she had a heart of gold and would do whatever it took.

In 1964 they received an award for being one of the most "typical farm families" in Illinois. The criteria for this honor was they were earning their living from the soil, raising a young family, and finding time for rural youth, 4H, church, and family activities. In all these the Bates family was "typical." The award was presented at the Illinois State Fair. That was a special memory that was fun for everyone.

The family had a garden on the farm. They would grow vegetables and sell them under the big tree in the front yard. One day Dave Clarke, a family friend who was a reporter for the Kewanee *Star Courier* newspaper, stopped out at the farm. He wrote a story about their vegetable business and called it "Verla's Veggies." I'm not so sure that wasn't what inspired Carol. She asked her employer at Sunnyfield Farm to use an extra five acres they had to plant a vegetable garden.

They grew way more vegetables than they could sell under the tree, so they started participating in the Farmer's Market held in Galesburg, Illinois. Every Saturday morning the family would head out at 4:00 a.m. to pick the vegetables so they would be fresh to sell. It was important that they sold a quality product. They would get to Main Street in Galesburg early to park the truck in a good spot. Then, set up the vegetables so everyone could see everything: tomatoes, green beans, squash, onions, pumpkins, and the favorite, sweet corn. They also sold yellow watermelons. These were green on the outside but yellow on the inside and people were intrigued. It was a long day but always a successful day because it was a family affair, so the cash box totals didn't matter.

Another family activity was making cinnamon rolls—one of Carol's specialties. They would fill the kitchen with them and then freeze to take to their friends and family in town.

The house this beautiful family lived in was a modest farmhouse, located a mile east of Galva on Route 34. It was always entered through the back door. Straight ahead were the steps to the basement and up a couple steps to the right brought you into the kitchen. There you found a huge oak table that filled the whole room—to sit at the far end you had to slide sideways to get to a chair. Beyond that was the galley kitchen, where there was always something cooking—usually meat and potatoes for whatever meal was next.

The family room had a linoleum floor with an area rug; Dad's recliner, Mom's rocker, and a sofa all faced the television set. The formal living room had red carpeting and a gun cabinet alongside the china cabinet. There was a narrow stairway next to the living room.

Upstairs were three bedrooms: the girls' room, the boys' room, and Carol and Ed's room. In the basement was a large room with a pool table. Carl loved to tell people he wasn't very good and watch their surprise when he'd beat them.

Outside was a small garage, a farrowing house where the baby pigs were born, a barn where the cattle were kept, a big metal shed for the machinery, a silo where they stored their corn, and a big yard to play.

Front Row L to R: Carl, Ernie, Verla
Back Row L to R: Carol, Judy, Ed

CHAPTER 3

Childhood

"Twenty years from now you'll be more disappointed by the things you didn't do than by the ones you did do. So throw off the bowlines. Sail away from the safe harbor. Catch the trade winds in your sails. Explore. Dream. Discover."
–Mark Twain

Carl loved to be outside; spring, summer, fall, and winter, he loved all the seasons. It was late in the fall the first time I knew that my job was not going to be easy. It was when Carl decided he needed to help his dad pick corn. Carl was around three years old and he was pulling his little red wagon across the busy highway. Mom was tending to the baby and lost sight of him. I had to think fast, so I got the attention of the traveler coming down the road and prompted him to stop and get Carl to safety. That was when Carl's passion for farming began and it never wavered. He was born to farm and this family farm was the perfect setting for his life.

He also loved raising cattle and hogs. It was satisfying watching the piglets grow and taking care of them until it was time to take them to the market. Oh, they made him mad sometimes when they didn't cooperate, but he loved the process. He and his cousins would talk for hours and hours about their cattle and their hogs. He loved working the fields every spring and fall.

With a houseful of kids and a family full of cousins, Ed and Carol decided to start a card club. It would prove to be entertainment for the adults after a hard week on the farm and a good time to get all the kids together.

Card club was a fun night in the Bates' home—Ed's brothers and sisters and a few other family friends would come to play euchre. At one gathering in particular I remember there being twelve adults and twenty-five children! The kids would go upstairs to play and this particular night Carl wanted to know what the grownups were talking and laughing about, so he leaned deep into the register and said, "Hi Mommy!" And then there he went, right through the register into the living room, landing on the sofa. I had to make sure Uncle Earl moved out of the way for that one!

Carl liked to play pranks and he and his boy cousins were always picking on the girls. I remember one night when they were army crawling down the hallway to sneak under one of the beds in the girls' room to scare them. Carl's mom was behind them carrying a yardstick. All of a sudden, the lights went on, the yardstick began swinging, and the boys were screaming and scrambling to get to their bedroom. I laughed and laughed, and so did the girls because the boys got in trouble.

Growing up, Carl did not go on many vacations—only two. They had animals to care for, camp every summer and the county fair, so there wasn't time to travel too far. The first one was when Ed decided to take Carl and Ernie and their cousin Roger to a baseball game to see the Chicago Cubs play. They were just pulling into the parking lot, which was quite a ways from the stadium, when they heard on the radio that a ball was hit into the wall and the outfielder was looking for it in the ivy. It was a historical event, the first ever "in park" home run. Carl remarked, in his matter-of-fact tone, "That was cool, wish we could've seen it."

The second vacation was to go see Busch stadium—Ed wasn't a Cardinals fan, but thought it would be nice for them to see the park, even though there was no game that day. Unfortunately, they arrived fifteen minutes after the team got done practicing. Carl leaned over the fence and one of the players gave him a bat. Ernie then leaned over, waiting to also get something. The player hesitantly handed a bat to Ernie and said, "Now listen, this bat is Bob Gibson's bat, and it's cracked so you can't use it." Ernie was mad because Carl could use his bat and he couldn't use the one he had received. Ed told him, "You might want to keep that bat." He still has it to this day. Sometimes we don't know how special are the gifts we receive.

Grandpa Bates' farm was also a great time for the cousins. The boys built an amazing fort behind the barn. To make sure that the girls would leave their fort alone, Carl told the girls that there was quicksand behind the barn. He told them that even cows were lost in the quicksand one year. He laid it on pretty thick about how dangerous it would be to walk back there. The girls never doubted his story and never came near their fort.

Twice a year the whole family—to include aunts, uncles, and cousins—would all get together. The family would have to rent spaces to have their summer family reunions and the Bates' Christmas. There were some great cooks in his family and everyone looked forward to the gatherings and the food that was plentiful and delicious. They could always count on the fresh raspberries on ice cream at the summer reunion and the popcorn balls at the Christmas gathering! These family traditions began in 1959 and continue to be passed on through the generations.

Sometimes there were gifts, even though they weren't that important to them. Staying connected and recognizing the gift of family was the best gift of all.

As Carl grew, he had no fear and he was no stranger to injuries—I did all I could to keep him as safe as possible. When he turned eight, Ed taught him how to drive the tractor; fortunately, he was pretty good at that. The red bicycle he got, however, was the source of a crash or two. Mom and Dad had bought it a little bigger so he could grow into it, but he'd ride so fast down the hill that he would crash into the side of the barn. It never fazed him; he'd get up, brush himself off, and do it again.

When Judy, Carl, Ernie, and Verla all had the chicken pox at the same time, I wondered how Carol was going to handle it. She had a brilliant idea and gave them all magic glasses that made the itching go away. Carl chose the red sunglasses. They really were magical because they all quit scratching when they had them on. Moms just know things!

As Ernie and Verla got older they were included in Judy and Carl's fun. It was always two against two but it always changed which two. The four of them loved making forts out of hay or playing flashlight tag—Carl was always the chief of the tribe and would wear his Daniel Boone hat and give them all duties. Carl always had the ideas but he would make the others do things first so he wouldn't get in trouble. If it looked fun he would join in. One game that could get pretty hysterical was when they would jump on the back of the pigs to see who could stay on the longest. There was that stinky puddle at the end of the pen they had to try and avoid. When they didn't avoid it, the other three would disappear because Mom wasn't going to be happy.

More jumping went on in the boys' bedroom where they had two beds—a twin and a full. The kids would turn on loud music and jump from one bed to the other. They thought the music covered their activity but the shaking lights downstairs told their parents what was going on. Carl did slip once and hit his head on a toy semi-truck. His eyebrow was cut pretty badly and there was blood everywhere. Mom quickly called the neighbor who was a nurse; she came right over and put a cold popsicle on his eyebrow, and let Carl open and eat one. Carl didn't cry, mostly because he wanted to be tough for his brother and sisters.

Carl's dad, Ed, taught the kids that working hard was important but playing was important too. He loved to make time to play baseball in the yard. Carl learned to work hard, play hard, and live life to the fullest. He was a Daddy's boy and Ed was a great role model. Ed heeded the advice of St. Francis of Assisi, "Preach the gospel and if necessary use words." His way of life was a testament to God's love. Ed didn't talk a lot but when he did, people listened. He taught Carl everything he knew about farming and about life. Carl never wanted to let his dad down.

Another thing Ed taught Carl was how to play cards. Ed loved to play cards and he was a serious player. If by chance his partner would make a not-so-strategic play, the silence was broken. Ed needed to speak and explain why that was not a good play and why they should not do it again. You had to be paying attention pretty closely when you were Ed's partner. Carl learned to be a competitive card player too. He was a risk taker—big surprise—and competitive.

One of Carl, Ernie, and Ed's favorite pastimes was watching the Cubs play baseball. They would lie on the living room floor, each with a bowl of ice cream—a traditional nightly treat—and watch the game. They would strategize how the Cubs could win. They always believed the World Series was possible for the Cubs, even though it had never happened in their lifetime. Ed taught the kids to love baseball and he coached Carl and Ernie's Little League teams. It turned out that Little League would prove to give Carl determination to overcome obstacles in his life.

Carl had a childhood full of love, laughter, hard work, and lessons learned. He wasn't perfect, that's for sure. Many times he would blame his siblings to avoid trouble for himself. Carl was a take-charge kind of guy, so he could be bossy. At the end of the day, Carl loved his family unconditionally. He always wanted what was best for them. He never wanted to be treated differently, but that's what happens sometimes in families.

As I said before, I love Carl, so the next chapter of his life was as hard for me as it was for him and his family. All of the previous injuries, near misses, and dangerous situations were nothing compared to what we were up against.

Carl at age 11

CHAPTER 4

St. Jude

"No child should die in the dawn of life."
—Danny Thomas

When God told me the news, I was devastated. I even questioned God, why Carl? He's such a leader for his siblings, he's such a help to his dad, and I went on and on! God told me that this family's faith would be tested, just like Abraham when he was asked to sacrifice his son, Isaac, in Genesis 22:1-18. God was confident that they would learn to trust in Him.

God said to me: "Gus, your job is to show Carl My love for him—don't let him doubt it for a minute, do you understand?" I said I did, and I really did. God was calling Carl to redemptive suffering, and while it was hard, I also knew that Carl's tenacity and stubbornness, along with his strong faith, would be a great example for all those around him both at this time and in the future! God uses the gifts people have to help others, even though they might not see the fruit of this until they get to their

Heavenly home. But when they get there it is all revealed, and the joy in seeing what an impact their life had in this earthly world is amazing!

Carl was playing in a 4H basketball game when he fell and hurt his leg. From that night on he was limping and experiencing a lot of pain. As brave and courageous as Carl had always been, his siblings could hear him crying at night because of the pain. It got to the point that he couldn't walk. Ed would carry him up to bed and down in the morning, while Carol was diligently trying to get answers to what was happening and causing her son to be in so much pain. The local doctor referred Carl to St. Jude's affiliate in Peoria, Illinois, where after many tests they found a sarcoma tumor on his lumbar spine. The growth was putting pressure to nerve sacs and paralyzing both legs.

Emergency surgery to remove this tumor was done at 2 a.m. on April 17, 1972. The best spinal surgeon at St. Jude Children's Research Hospital in Memphis was flown in. The surgery was not a guarantee—the doctors really didn't think there was any chance of survival, but felt like they had to do something. Someone even referred to it as a Hail Mary surgery. I was praying for Carl and his whole family to have peace and strength.

The family heard there was a twenty-three-year-old patient with the same cancer; the doctors had tried the same surgery and he did not make it. The doctors explained that if he survived he probably would never walk again. But at 2 a.m. nobody cared about any of that, and Ed and Carol knew that Carl had grit! He didn't give up, he didn't complain, he gave it his all, no matter what. They prayed and trusted and he survived.

Nobody in the family said the word "cancer," and they only talked about the time "when Carl got to come home."

Some kids at school told Judy that her brother was going to die from cancer. Her guardian angel, Calvin, made sure she continued believing in miracles and God's love for her and for Carl.

At the hospital, Carl had to have bone marrow tests to look for cancer in other areas. It was a very painful procedure. Carl then volunteered to hold the hands of other younger kids while they had to have those tests. I was so proud of his giving heart. Focusing on helping others was lessening the fear he was feeling.

We were in the hospital for seven weeks with six days in intensive care. Once he was out of intensive care, Carl would be wheeled down to the playroom every day before or after treatments. He would meet kids and they would play board games or cards. When some of his new friends weren't coming anymore, the nurses would tell Carl that they went home. Carl knew what that really meant.

Every day was something new. The nurse brought some wigs for Carl to look at, to prepare for when his hair would fall out. Carl threw the wigs across the room—he was not going to lose his hair, he said, and by gosh it only thinned a bit. God was happy to oblige. Sometimes people think that God only wants to hear the big problems, but He loves when His children ask even for little things, like hair.

As the days went by, many procedures were necessary to diagnose and treat the disease. At each new test, Carl would ask what they were going to do and was it going to hurt. If they didn't tell him the truth he would get mad, so they didn't try to pull anything over on him. He never let anyone know that he was afraid.

He was stubborn and knew that he was going to play Little League again—that was his focus! He believed it and that attitude is what pushed him forward. He would lie and imagine himself pitching or hitting the ball, running the bases, giving high fives when he made a home run.

After the surgery, he had to learn to walk for the second time in his life. To accomplish this, they would strap him onto a metal table, tip it to get him in a standing position, and then start his physical therapy. He was determined. They had told him he probably wouldn't be able to walk, but that only made him more committed to prove them wrong. It took a while, but within those seven weeks he was able to walk out of the hospital.

Carl was very inspired by Danny Thomas, who gave his whole life to help children. Danny Thomas had asked St. Jude, the saint for hopeless causes, to show him where his life should go. The St. Jude Children's Research Hospital was born from that prayer. When Carl met Danny, he told Carl "never give up." He also told Carl that God put him on earth to live.

Carl knew that he was experiencing a miracle. He loved his chats with Father John from Africa and the hospital chaplain, Pastor Johnson, who came every day. Little did Carl know that he was being an inspiration to all of them as much as they were to him. His total peace and confidence blessed them.

The community, his Little League team, and his classmates sending him cards kept his spirits up. He was so appreciative. He wrote a heartfelt thank-you and sent it to the *Galva News*, the local newspaper, to be published for all of the community to see. It went as follows:

Dear Galvans:

Five weeks I've been in Peoria Methodist Hospital. It hasn't been five weeks of fun but I still am working toward the day to be back playing ball with all my friends. It will sure be nice to see everyone again and I know the time is coming. I want to send a special thanks to everyone for the many cards and gifts. I cannot begin to tell you how grateful I am. The fund started by the First United Methodist Church in Galva can never be forgotten by myself and my family. The prayers I know will be with me a lifetime. With Rev. Metzger and all my Sunday school teachers' training, I know God will take care of me. I send a prayer back to all of you, "that no matter how rough the going, God is there so trust in him." I am a Cubs fan and somewhere I have a special friend that told the Cubs team about me. They sent me a personally signed ball and I will remember this for years. I have my Little League uniform hanging in my room. The teachers in school back home have been great helping the students writing letters. Thanks kids. Mr. Patterson my principal sent me a letter after looking at my work, so guess what friends: I'll be in the seventh grade! The doctors and nurses have more plans for me today so I must close. Hoping the Galva News will print my thank you. Last but not least, people must be proud to have a newspaper like the Galva News, a special thank you Mr. Holding and crew.

From your friend, Carl Bates

Then, a two-year journey began. He received a total of thirty cobalt radiation treatments and chemotherapy every other Friday for those two years. I hated that he would throw up on the trip home after each treatment. His last treatment was scheduled for May 2, 1974, and he looked forward to no more medicine.

The first Sunday after Carl came home, his family went to the second service at the First United Methodist Church. He was presented with another special baseball. It was sent to him from the parents of Rev. Metzger, the pastor at the church. They lived in Williamsport, Pennsylvania, where the world Little League tournament was held each August. It was hit by one of the Little Leaguers who made a home run. It was autographed by the president of Little League with best wishes to Carl. They invited Carl and his family to come to Pennsylvania, but life on the farm doesn't leave much time for traveling.

God's love was flowing from all of these people. I was aware of a special lady in town who cut the article about Carl out of the paper and put it in her scrapbook and prayed for him, even though she didn't know him or his family. She would get to know him very well years later.

As a celebration gift for his return home, he received a black-and-red minibike. You know that old saying, "Don't drive faster than your guardian angel can go" . . . well he tried to go faster! Carl was back to normal, feeling blessed, feeling free, and his brother and sisters loved having him back home. Funny thing about that minibike, Ed could be seen taking it out to check the fields every now and then. His long legs made it a comical sight.

In August, Carl was excited to be able to show his hogs at the fair. He knew it was a miracle that he was not going to miss one single 4H show. Carl's pediatrician, Dr. Robert Hart from Peoria, came to that fair as he had promised. He told Carl that when he got better he would come to his 4H show. He purchased Carl's hog at a very hefty price to prove to Carl how proud he was of his efforts and attitude to get better. At the show, Carl was still a little unsteady with his walking and would fall often, but he would say, "No time to cry about it, just got to keep going."

He had also been able to attend 4H camp, with Judy there to keep an eye on him and make sure he didn't overdo it. We had our work cut out for us. Carl was finally old enough to go on the overnight hike called The Primitive. Judy was going, along with her friend, Ann, and her little sister, Wendy. Everyone had to carry all the supplies they could to a remote site. The youth had to dig latrines, make a fire, set up a camp, and pitch the tents. Carl wasn't allowed to carry anything or help with the digging. It was a secret from everyone on the hike as to why. Carl didn't want any special attention or for anyone to feel sorry for him, and insisted no one would know about his cancer. They foraged and cooked the food they found and brought. The counselors had brought a guitar and they sang around the campfire, told jokes, and listened to scary stories until late into the night. It was a magical night under a beautiful sky and Carl felt like a normal kid again.

I was so happy that Carl had persevered through this trial, and he never lost hope. I helped him see the miracle that God had given him. He was grateful and ready to live.

CHAPTER 5

Adolescence

"Like a true nature's child we were born, born to be wild."
—Steppenwolf

Carl's first job, besides helping his dad, was for Heinold Hog Market. Willy Stewart hired him to castrate hogs. After a couple days, he asked Willy if he could get his brother, Ernie, to help him. He agreed and so Ernie came the next day. Carl instructed Ernie to catch and hold the hog while he zapped it. His workday got a lot easier, and Ernie made a few dollars.

When it came to Ernie, it seemed Carl always made him do the hard stuff. At the time, Ernie probably thought it was so Carl could get out of it. But Carl wasn't lazy; it was God's way of teaching Ernie to be strong, to take things seriously, and to be the successful man he turned out to be. I think sometimes Ernie was torn between feeling jealous for the attention Carl got and feeling how unfair it was that Carl had to endure so many problems. Ernie proved to have a huge heart. As a child,

Carl said Ernie had big eyes, but later in life, Carl saw his heart was even bigger.

Carl continued to be active in 4H. He had shown hogs at the Henry County Fair from the age of eight to seventeen. He spent a week every summer at 4H camp and it was obvious that agriculture was in his blood. The friends he met at camp loved Carl's humor and adventurous nature. Dad would help Carl with his 4H projects, but usually let Carl do things his own way first—and then if it didn't work out, he would show him another way. Ed was helping Carl gain confidence and learn by trial and error.

In 1976, Carl's 4H project included a report titled, "My Journey Through Cancer." I loved his openness to share this story with his club members.

Carl would make extra money working for other farmers baling hay in the summers. He and his friend, Dan Brooks, would also go trapping. Every Saturday morning they would sell the animal hides to the buyer who would come to town. He loved to mess with Judy's and Verla's friends by asking them to go down to the basement and get ice cream from the upright freezer. When they'd open it they'd find his dead animals that he had caught trapping.

He saved everything he made until he was able to buy a brand-new royal blue Camaro Z28. He was so proud but I had to be on my best game—that car was fast!

As Carl became a teenager, he liked to cause trouble. It was that mischievous look in his eye from the beginning. Mother Bates, as she was called, always blamed Carl's siblings and friends for any trouble they got into, but Carl and I knew who started it all.

I'll never forget the time when a bunch of guys stayed all night at the hog barn before the Henry County Fair show. Carl and his cousin decided to get some beer. They scoped out the bunch and decided Mike looked the oldest, but still lacked a bit of maturity, so they cut some hair from a cow's tail and glued it to Mike's upper lip in the shape of a moustache. Mike got the beer but he had one heck of a time getting rid of the makeshift moustache. Mike had chosen a malt liquor beer for their first drinking alcohol experience. Carl vowed to get the beer himself next time. He thought that it was terrible, which kept them from drinking too much of it!

Another time, they heard the police coming to raid the barn for underage drinking, and they all crawled out the windows onto the roof. Never a dull moment!

The Galva Sodbusters was the name of the 4H group Carl and his brother, Ernie, were in. Every year they had a variety show that all the area 4H groups would come to and show their talents. It was called Share the Fun. One year Ernie was the MC and there were some technical difficulties, so he sang a solo while they corrected the problem. His song of choice was "The Battle of New Orleans." It was the only song he could remember the words to. He belted out the chorus as he slapped his knee to the beat. Ernie could always keep the party going with his gift of entertainment.

That was the same year there was a girl named Pam who participated in a song and dance routine to "Matchmaker" from *Fiddler on the Roof*. When the number was over, Pam found herself on the outside of the curtain—she was so embarrassed as she tried to find the opening to get backstage! That's when Carl first noticed her. He would remember that later.

Life on the farm could be entertaining also. When Carl needed help on the farm, he thought it was fun to ask his townie friends. So when it was time to castrate hogs, he called Kent. Unaccustomed to farm-work, Kent would get close to the little pigs and they would bolt away, and so in frustration he tried diving to catch one. He landed on an electric fence that was live. After a couple jolts he rolled off the wire. Carl was laughing so hard they had to take a break. Every time Carl would see Kent, the story would resurface and Carl would laugh just as hard.

Later that same day when Verla came home from basketball practice she couldn't get out of her car. Carl was throwing the pig testicles at the car—he loved to laugh and make people laugh. It was a gift from God that he recognized and used to its full potential.

Another funny story was when his cousin, Roger, whom they nicknamed Pooh, had come over and they had gone out to the hog house. The top of the half door was closed to keep the wind out, but the hogs were all lying down looking peaceful. Roger commented, "Do you think I could go sit on one?" Carl said, "Sure, why not! They won't move." Roger sat gently on one of the sleeping hogs but it immediately jumped up, ran through the half door, and knocked him off just like in a cartoon. We had so much fun on the farm.

Carl had some friends over one night and they had a party in the hog lot. The next day his dad was moving hogs to that field and found a bunch of empty beer cans in one of the A-frame hog houses. He asked Carl if he knew where they came from and Carl told him that he saw some vagrants out there the day before. I know Ed didn't believe him but Mother Bates believed it as gospel. I made sure Ed was aware of what Carl and his friends were up to, so that he would keep his eye on them.

Another friend of Carl's was around quite a bit. His name was Bill and he felt like part of the family. Bill had lost his dad when he was in his mid-teens and Ed was there for Bill to keep him in line and give him advice. One night, Carl talked Bill into crashing a party—I knew it wasn't a good idea but Carl wasn't listening to me. Carl, Bill, and their friend Joe went to meet some of the girls at the party, but the boys didn't appreciate these party crashers. All of a sudden the room went dark and a fight broke out. Carl ended up with a chipped tooth and Bill had a large shiner. The next morning, Bill stopped out at the farm where Carl met him at the door to save him from the wrath of Mom and Dad Bates. Ed followed Carl outside and chatted with Bill for a little bit. Bill held his breath the whole time hoping he wouldn't ask him to take off the sunglasses.

Now that Carl was starting to get interested in girls, I knew there was one who was interested in him and was perfect for him. Pam saw him in the school hall one day wearing gray corduroy pants and a two-tone gray rugby shirt. She asked a friend who he was as she thought he was cute. God definitely gives us free will when it comes to choosing a boy or girl to date and eventually marry. But he also puts people in our lives that he knows would be good for us, and that we would be good for.

Pam always picked Carl in PE class during the square dancing unit. Carl had his own rhythm and he loved to dance, and Pam followed along just perfectly. Imagine him dancing when they never thought he would even walk. God's grace! He asked her one day if he could come over and see her that night. She said yes, but when he wouldn't tell his mom where he was going, she wouldn't let him have the car.

Their first date was March 12, 1977. After a school dance, Carl drove Pam home. He asked if he could kiss her good night—such a gentleman. That was the beginning of their long-lasting relationship. Carl was a junior and Pam was a sophomore at Galva High School. They went to all school functions and dances as a couple. They had many double dates with Carl's friends Joe and Bill and their girlfriends. They both also spent time with friends, but they knew from the beginning they had a special bond and loved spending time together. I knew it was meant to be. There were a few breakups along the way, but they never lasted more than a few weeks. Absence did make the heart grow fonder.

Soon after Carl's senior year of school started, he was in a serious motorcycle accident. That motorcycle was the source of a lot of stress for me and all those who loved him. He refused to listen to me and did not slow down—ever. He flew over the hood of a classmate's car and gashed his head open and hurt his leg. This scared him but not for too long. Another close call, but again he survived.

Carl graduated high school with awards from FFA and 4H. He played intramural basketball, Babe Ruth baseball, and worked on the farm with his dad. He then attended Black Hawk East College in nearby Kewanee, Illinois, and graduated with an associate degree in Agriculture. He met new friends through a basketball league and the numerous college parties.

After Pam graduated, she moved to the Quad City area to attend college. It was only an hour away, but Carl missed her a lot. This was a difficult time for their relationship. He always wondered if she would be faithful, and this jealousy was what became an obstacle. One night when she came home for the weekend, they fought and ended up in a car accident. Carl, Carl, Carl! His car was damaged extensively but Pam and Carl survived with minor injuries.

On one of Carl's friend's bachelor parties, they went to some pretty raunchy establishments. I coaxed Carl to make some trouble and they got kicked out. We can use whatever means are necessary per the Boss! After they left, they went to a party of someone they had met that night. Carl saw a garden hose near someone's car and decided that it would be funny to fill their car with water. He put the hose in the window and turned the water on. Then Carl told his friends it was time to go. They didn't necessarily want to but could see that Carl wasn't taking no for an answer. Carl could not pass up a good prank, unfortunately for the recipient of his antics.

This time in his life was a struggle for me to keep him safe and on the right track. The parties were constant. One night in particular I had to wake Ed up to check on him. He heard Carl come home and then looked outside. When Carl came in he asked him if he'd been drinking—Carl answered no. He asked him again and Carl said no. The third time Carl answered no, Ed told him to go out to the hog lot, shut his car off, and shut the car door.

I know that getting caught made an impact on Carl. He'd lied to his dad and felt like he'd let him down. Ed was forgiving and made sure Carl knew he still loved him. God our father knows His children don't always make the best choices, but His love is unconditional too.

Nothing we do can separate us from the love of God, as it states in scripture:

"For I am convinced that neither death, nor life, nor angels, nor principalities, nor present things, nor future things, nor powers, nor height, nor depth, nor any other creature will be able to separate us from the love of God in Christ Jesus our Lord." (Romans 8:38-39)

Carl at the 4H Henry County Fair

Carl & Steve King at one of the many parties.

CHAPTER 6

Pam

*"So they are no longer two, but one flesh. Therefore, what
God has joined together, no human being must separate."*
(Matthew 19:6)

In the winter of 1979, Carl and some buddies went on a ski trip to Chestnut Mountain in Galena, Illinois. Carl took one trip down the slope and wiped out pretty badly. Fortunately I was able to get the message across that a fall could injure his spine, and he went to the lodge to wait for his buddies to finish skiing. He would never want to ruin their fun. This gave him a lot of time to think about his life, his plans, and goals.

It was that trip when Carl decided that Pam was the girl he wanted to marry. Being apart had been very stressful and they talked about Pam coming back to Galva and getting a job at the dentist office, where she had worked during high school.

However, while Carl was convinced that Pam was the girl he wanted to spend the rest of his life with, he had some concerns. I was aware of these reservations but I also knew what Pam's feelings were. You see, Carl had been told that because of his cobalt radiation treatments as a child, it was probable that he would not be able to father children. That weighed heavily on his heart; would Pam be okay with not having children? Would he be enough?

At this same time, Pam was discerning what she wanted and was contemplating breaking up. This separation was wearing on their relationship. Sam, her guardian angel, knew that was not God's plan and sent her a message as she was preparing to move home for the summer. "GO HOME to CARL" was the message that played over and over in her head, and she heard it in her heart. It was like a weight had been lifted and she knew this relationship was meant to be. She also knew this was a God-incidence.

I had spoken with Sam and he told me what Pam's feelings were. Together we were determined to break down the obstacles to their union. You see, Pam had suffered a great loss when she was thirteen years old.

It was early in the morning on a school day. Pam and her two sisters, Paula and Leigh, got up and went downstairs to have breakfast. They heard their ten-month-old baby sister, Jennifer, talking in her crib but she seemed happy and content so they left her there. When Pam got back upstairs she went to Jennifer's room to get her up. Jennifer loved to hang out with the girls as they got dressed for school. Pam found Jennifer lifeless in her crib. The string she had around her neck with her pacifier attached had gotten caught on the knob that pulled the side of the crib up and down. Jennifer had fallen and strangled. Pam lifted her out of the crib and became hysterical and chaos ensued. Pam's mom, Cheryl, was trying to perform CPR and Pam's sister Paula called the ambulance, but the ambulance service had just switched from the funeral home to a separate provider so she called the wrong number. The funeral director knew that something was terribly wrong and he contacted the ambulance and came over himself to see if he could be of assistance.

Jennifer left this world that day and was born into eternal life. By God's grace, the life insurance policy that Pam's parents had purchased when she was born had just been signed the day before with the neighbor, who had stopped by as a witness. Uncle Wally, the insurance agent, had just gotten around to it. Without a witness, the policy would not have paid for her funeral. The catastrophe prompted new labeling on pacifiers with a warning about putting them on a string around baby's necks, so this would be avoided in the future. The love that surrounded the family was overwhelming. God was orchestrating good to come from this heartbreaking event.

What no one knew was that Pam was having nightmares for months. In these dreams, Jennifer would die in different scenarios—choking, falling, drowning, and the dream would always end with her holding Jennifer's lifeless body. Pam did not share these dreams with anyone, as she knew everyone was going through their own grieving process. She felt she now knew the pain of losing a child and she didn't ever want to experience that again. Sam prompted Pam to share this fear with Carl, so he knew that she was okay with not having children if that was God's plan.

Christmas Eve 1980, he gave Pam a note that she could pick out any ring she wanted. They went shopping at Zales and she picked out a marquise diamond. On Valentine's Day they set the date: September 19, 1981.

They proceeded to take pre-cana classes through the Catholic Church, and it was determined that they were compatible and were given the blessing of the priest. Pam and Carl both answered *Agree* to the question: "I am sure that I will never doubt my love for my future husband/wife." And *Disagree* to the question: "One cannot be absolutely sure that his/her choice of a mate is correct." They were committed to living out this vocation of marriage for life.

The wedding was held at the First United Methodist Church where Carl attended. Father Ron Palmer from St. Mary's Catholic Church also assisted in the ceremony.

Carl was dared to wear tennis shoes to the wedding and was bet $50 he wouldn't do it. Pam knew Carl well enough that she went out and bought him new gray tennis shoes that matched his tux. The photographer wasn't amused and painstakingly made sure most of the pictures had his shoes behind Pam's dress. His friend, Dougie, paid his debt!

After the wedding and reception, Carl's brother, Ernie, surprised them with a room at a local hotel. They were not expecting to stay overnight so they did not have a change of clothes. Driving through McDonald's the next morning for breakfast with their wedding dress and tux was probably quite a sight.

They were excited to settle into life as husband and wife. For a few months, they lived in an apartment in town, and then heard that the farmhouse just a mile down from his family home was for rent. They called and moved to the farm on Christmas Day, 1981.

In the beginning of their marriage, Carl worked as a hired hand for Chuck Anderson and also helped his dad. He slowly started buying his own equipment and livestock in hopes he could farm on his own someday.

Life on the farm brought many adventures. There was an accident on the highway during a snowstorm. Pam opened the door to a young man bleeding profusely from a cut on his neck. I knew this was serious and prayed both Carl and Pam would feel God's peace in helping this man. Pam used all of their towels to put pressure on his neck to stop the bleeding and made conversation to keep him awake. He told her he was a wrestler from the Chicago area and they were headed to Waunee Farm for their grandparents' anniversary party. Carl had to run down to the accident site to get the ambulance crew to come back to the house. When they got this young man in the ambulance he went into shock. He was taken to the nearby hospital where he was treated for a lacerated carotid artery and survived. The family stopped by the farm several weeks later to thank Pam and Carl and offered to pay them. They told them they wouldn't accept anything and would hope someone would help them if they were ever in need. Paying it forward is such a beautiful response.

Carl loved all of his friends, but he also loved playing jokes on them! Some of his friends got a bathtub full of Jell-O or a decorated car when they got married. But if anyone needed anything, Carl was there for them. He was a loyal and good friend to everyone he met. His friends were lifelong friends—the kind that you might not see for years, but when you get together it's like you were never apart.

Remembering his childhood, they started a card club. The group drew for partners and played five-point pitch. Carl always bid, no matter what. It was a challenge to be his partner. He'd give that mischievous smile and most times make the bid, and if he didn't, he'd blame his partner.

At one of their New Year's Eve parties, everyone was asked to do some sort of entertainment, skit, etc. There were many hysterical portrayals from TV sitcoms. Then when things had quieted down and all the skits were over, Carl got up and started running through the house as fast as he could go while everyone sat in wonderment of what he was doing. He stopped, sat down, and announced: "Life in the Fast Lane." That was Carl!

There was a birthday celebration for Pam and Paula one year that included a treasure hunt. Each clue was in the form of a poem and the clues were hidden all over Galva and the surrounding area. All of the guests were sent out in teams to find the clues. The police department was alerted so nobody would get in trouble. The drivers were not adhering very well to the rules of the road or speed limits. There were a lot of guardian angels working hard to keep everyone safe. First team back to the house won!

Carl and Pam also had a lot of friends through Carl's slow-pitch softball team—Carl was a pitcher on this team. The team sponsors started with The Jug and then when that bar closed they became Bud's Place and then Colony Inn. It was a crazy time. Most of the tournaments they entered also had a drinking contest along with the softball. It seemed that the team cared more about winning the drinking contest than the softball games. The summers were filled with games and tournaments. This team of friends also planned activities to do together besides playing softball. There were many trips to Chicago on the train to see Cubs or White Sox games. Their biggest trip was when everyone went to Lake of the Ozarks and they rented a houseboat. It was such a great time. Jay Halsall was the team captain and planned these activities to keep his team connected. Shortly after that Ozark trip, Jay was killed in a car accident. I knew this impacted Carl and made him reevaluate his life and priorities, as did many of the other team members. God was close to all of them as they grieved their friend. He is always at our side. God tells us "Blessed are they who mourn, for they will be comforted." (Matthew 5:4)

Early in their marriage, Carl wanted to share one of his joys of farming with Pam. Hogs were a big part of Carl's farming operation. Baby pigs being born was a process. As the mothers sometimes wanted to eat their babies, it was important to move them away for a time. Pam was a townie and basically afraid of animals, but she wanted to be helpful to her new husband. He asked if she would come out and help. She didn't realize that meant taking the slippery newborn baby pigs and wiping them off with straw. She was out of her comfort zone for sure. Carl was cutting the umbilical cords and threw one that wrapped around her leg. Now she was hysterical, but what was worse was Carl was laughing! This made her think he did it on purpose. This was the last time she offered to help on the farm when animals were involved. She did take an occasional ride on a tractor or combine.

Pam learned that being a farmer's wife meant sacrifice and commitment. During the spring planting and fall harvest she was alone for days and nights at a time. This was the life God chose for them and trusted it was all for good. "Let us not grow tired of doing good, for in due time we shall reap our harvest, if we do not give up." (Galatians 6:9) .

Even though Pam was not your typical farmwife, she loved that Carl loved what he was doing. She loved her job at the dental office and life was good.

God brings all kinds of people together—in some marriages the partners are a lot alike, and in some they are very different. Love and commitment are what make it work. Pam and Carl made the decision to be together until death; it was a covenant with God that they took very seriously.

1978 Prom

Carl's wedding shoes

Pam and Carl 2015

Front Row: Dan Brooks, Bill Johnson, Kent Norman, Jay Halsall, Ron Ivie 2nd Row: Bud Bates, Royce Johnson Back Row: Denny Tarleton, John Stephenson, Joe Novotny, Doug Wilsey, Carl, Dougie Anderson

CHAPTER 7

The In-Laws

"Blood makes you related, loyalty makes you family."
—Anonymous

Carl married into a loud family. He admitted during his wedding prep classes that they scared him a little. If the lyrics or title of a song are mentioned at a family gathering in conversation, it's not uncommon to hear them all join into a sing-along. You could say "they are making a joyful noise" more than "they are a musical family!" God gives us all different gifts. Carl would just smirk and shake his head. Because they all lived in Galva, it's who they spent most of their time with.

His father-in-law was John and mother-in-law, Cheryl. They were high school sweethearts. Cheryl moved to Illinois from Arizona her freshman year of high school and they started dating her sophomore year. John was a very shy guy as a young man but after taking a Dale Carnegie sales class he spent the rest of his life selling things—from soap to insurance. He loved to strike up conversations with people and when he was called to the deaconate he especially loved sharing God's love with others. Just as Peter was a fisher of men in God's plan, Deacon John was a salesman for God. John and Cheryl enjoyed bringing new Catholics into the church through teaching the RCIA classes (Rite of Christian Initiation of Adults).

Cheryl was a stay-at-home mom when the children were growing up. Later she had several jobs in real estate and car sales.

John and Cheryl always thought the world of Carl. They knew he was good for Pam.

Carl also gained many new grandmothers. Both Cheryl's mom and grandmother were still living. Great Grandma Lillian Miner had come to America when she was just eight years old from Sweden. She had a picture of Carl cut from the newspaper in her scrapbook, from when he was battling cancer. The family found it after her death. That was years before Pam even knew Carl. Was that a sign that Pam and Carl were meant to be together? God does give us clues if we are paying attention—another God-incidence. Christmas Eve was always held at Great Grandma Lillian's house. Carl came the first year he and Pam were dating and never missed another one. It was after one of these celebrations that he proposed.

Grandma Dorothea Ericson, Cheryl's mom, was always concerned about Carl. Was he eating enough, did he get enough sleep during the busy times on the farm? She didn't like that he didn't eat many vegetables. Maybe that five-acre vegetable garden had something to do with that? She would make different ones for him to try at every family gathering. She was the school cafeteria cook for two generations and loved to prepare most of the holiday meals. She offered Carl lima beans at one of those dinners and he said they weren't bad. I laughed because the family had lima beans for every family gathering from then on.

Grandma Darlene Holevoet, John's mom, was Carl's card partner. If nobody else wanted to play, those two would play themselves. Darlene worked at the veterinary office in Galva pretty much her whole life. She lost her husband to throat cancer when she was in her late thirties. She loved to bowl and fish and play bingo, besides playing cards. When she got older and couldn't get around very well, Carl was always looking out for her. Grandma Darlene always made Carl his favorite cake: chocolate cake with white fluffy frosting.

Pam was an identical twin. Her twin sister, Paula, tried once to fool Carl. When he came to pick Pam up for a date, Paula jumped in his car and he immediately knew. He said, "Hi Paula, where's Pam?" Carl had a way of greeting people that Paula especially loved. He would say their name in a singsong voice, dragging out the first syllable, "Paaaaauuuula!" He was like a big brother to her and gave good advice, whether she wanted it or not.

Pam and Paula were best friends. They fought and argued but at the end of the day they had a bond that couldn't be broken.

Paula married Keith (Lou) Patty the year before Pam and Carl were married. Carl and Lou became very close over the years. They played softball together, and due to the closeness of Pam and Paula spent a lot of time together.

Pam's younger sister, Leigh—pronounced Lay, like the potato chip—was always pestering Pam and Carl when they were dating. But Carl always stuck up for her.

After losing their daughter, Jennifer, John and Cheryl decided to have another child. That's when they had their first boy.

Rich, Pam's brother, was a toddler when Carl started dating Pam. Carl loved watching Richie learn new things. As he grew, Richie loved to hang out on the farm, so Carl hired him to walk the bean field and pull weeds. He paid him $1 a row. It took him all day to do two rows, so it was a win-win for Carl. Richie decided to look for another career path.

Carl grew to love his extended family. On occasion he even joined in with the family sing-along. They didn't scare him anymore.

CHAPTER 8

Growing Family

*"Miracles happen every day, change your perception of
what a miracle is and you'll see them all around you."*
—Jon Bon Jovi

In January 1982, Pam and Carl got word of another miracle
in their lives. Despite all the cobalt radiation and chemo
treatments, Pam was pregnant. Pam and Carl were beside
themselves with joy; they knew that God had the perfect plan
and had given them a gift. Carl never expected the miracle of
children. I was so excited for them. His friend Bill and wife,
Ellie, were expecting at the same time so they shared rides
to Lamaze classes and went out for Godfather's pizza after.
In the class, Carl was told that Pam and he would be so in
tune that during labor when he snapped his fingers Pam would
be put at ease. Pam developed high blood pressure and spent
a week in the hospital prior to delivery. When she went into
labor, Carl kept snapping his fingers until Pam told him to
stop or she would cut them off! Tara Marie Bates was born on

September 4, 1982, a perfect little girl who looked just like her daddy. They took Tara to Dr. Hart—Carl's childhood doctor—in Peoria and he was amazed. He confirmed that she was a miracle.

Carl took parenting as an equal with Pam. He changed diapers, fed, bathed, and watched her when Pam had somewhere to go. Carl understood fatherhood was a gift—a miracle in his case—and he was engaged to be the best dad he could be.

Paula and Lou had Heather about a year before Tara was born. She was a twin; her sister Dena, however, only lived three hours. Dena was born without a diaphragm. Because of Paula and Lou's willingness to let them do an autopsy, advancements have been made to correct that problem in utero. She went to Heaven with Carl's sister Carrie and Pam's sister Jennifer, and they were all great prayer warriors with special purpose. Heather and Tara were close friends growing up, like sisters really.

In late 1985, Pam's guardian angel, Sam, and I gave Carl and Pam the nudge to try for another child. Along came miracle number two, Tyler Carl Bates, on September 26, 1986. He was a big baby like his daddy at 9 lbs. 7 oz. and also looked just like him. They took him to Dr. Hart as well, and he was even more surprised. He told them he really thought Tara was a fluke—this was another true miracle.

Tara was just like another mommy to Tyler. Her favorite toys were her baby dolls and now she had a real live one! They were close growing up and always looked out for each other.

Jake, Paula and Lou's son, was just a year older than Tyler. Jake and Tyler were a comedy act growing up. Carl surprised them one night when he was watching them. The usually mild-mannered Carl had hit his limit with their shenanigans and told them if they did whatever they were doing one more time, he was going to get them. They couldn't control themselves and did it again. Carl jumped up and they ran and locked themselves in the bathroom for most of the evening. He never would have hurt them but they knew he meant business. Now, I'm not saying Carl was never angry or disappointed with people. That is human nature, but he knew not to hold onto it. Many times as guardian angels we speak the words *let it go*.

Brynn came along later—sixteen years later. Paula and Lou knew that God's plan is always perfect! She loved her Uncle Carwee as she referred to him. Carl took her on the combine every fall and gave her rides on the mule around the yard. He loved her like a grandchild and spoiled her like one too.

Pam's sister Leigh moved away for many years—she lived down south in Alabama and Georgia. Her husband, Kenny, was in the Army. When Leigh and Kenny divorced, she moved back to Galva with her little girl, Cassie. She opened a restaurant/ice cream joint called The Dairy Barn. Carl had his usual every day: cheeseburger, french fries, and a Pepsi. He was their best customer and sometimes Cassie would go with him to help him farm after his lunch.

Pam's brother, Rich, grew up to be a bit of a wild child. But God didn't give up on him either. God doesn't give up on any of us. Jesus died for every single person. It's our response, our surrender that determines our future. Rich chose God's plan for his life and eventually he, like his dad, also was ordained a deacon in the Catholic Church. Rich married Jennifer, whom he met through a mutual friend. They had a daughter, Lily, and live in the Chicago area where Jennifer's family lived.

Carl's family was growing also. Judy was the first to leave home. She went to Bradley University in Peoria, Illinois. She met Chris there, and they married and had three children: Cullen, Chris, and Clay. They lived in Texas, Florida, and settled in Wisconsin.

Ernie started at Black Hawk College and then transferred to University of Illinois. He met Sarah, and it was love at first sight. They married and moved near her family in Lanark, Illinois. They also had three children: Taylor, Blair, and Parker.

Verla attended Bradley University like her sister. Shortly after graduation, she moved to Atlanta, Georgia, where she met her husband, Scott. They had two children: Paul and Erin.

The Bates family stayed close. They always showed up for special events and especially Christmas Day, which was Carol's birthday. God loves for families to stick together; it's by His divine plan that we are given the family that we have. It is important to make an effort to get along. Forgiveness is the key—people are going to do things and say things that might make us angry or sad. Holding on to that anger or grief just eats away at our soul. It's like weeds growing and taking over the crop until there is little left to harvest.

Through Carl's life experiences he grasped this lesson. He never had ill feelings toward others and lived his life with love in his heart for his friends and family.

I loved being a part of this family and watching them love each other the best that they could.

Carl and Brynn Patty

CHAPTER 9

Beautiful Life

"The love of a family is life's greatest blessing."
—Eva Burrows

Sharing in the daily lives of Carl's family brought glory to God and joy to me. I loved being there and watching the blessings flow.

Pam worked part-time at the dental office after Tara was born. When Tara was two years old, she had the opportunity to become the office manager and went to full-time. Carl started renting farm ground and doing custom combining. Carl always had an entrepreneurial mind-set. He loved spending time in the combine, so it was a win-win for him and for the farmers who didn't want to purchase their own combine. The custom work grew quickly so Carl stopped working for Chuck.

Money was sometimes tight, but Carl had aspirations to have good equipment. He saw the bigger picture, while Pam saw the immediate struggle. Carl knew that risk was involved to grow. He understood the trust needed in the farming industry.

When Peter saw Jesus walking on the water, he said, "Lord, if it is you, command me to come to you on the water." He said, "Come." Peter got out of the boat and began to walk on the water toward Jesus. But when he saw how strong the wind was he became frightened; and, beginning to sink, he cried out, "Lord, save me!" Immediately Jesus stretched out his hand and caught him, and said to him, "O you of little faith, why did you doubt?" (Matthew 14:28-31)

Carl didn't doubt. He had confidence and perseverance—virtues that served him well. He would get up every morning, usually wear some crazy t-shirt with some crazy saying on it, and trust that God and I would guide him through his day.

As Tara and Tyler became toddlers, he would let them tag along when he was working, whether taking care of the pigs or working in the fields—they were always welcome to watch from the truck or ride in the combine or tractor. He was a hard worker and it was good for the kids to see that. His confidence, stoic nature, and humility always made everyone feel comfortable.

Carl also loved being the cook in the family. He'd create all kinds of recipes. It usually started with frying up some hamburger and throwing various things in with it, but it was always topped with cheese. "Carl's Surprise" and a Pepsi was Tara and Tyler's favorite meal. For Carl anything was good with a Pepsi!

I was proud of Carl when he agreed to serve his community as the president of the rural fire protection district. He held the position from 1989 to 2015. The volunteer fire department was something Galva could be proud of. Carl was instrumental in getting them the equipment they needed to keep Galvans safe. It may seem like a small contribution, but people willing to give of their time, talent, or treasure make the world a better place.

One of Carl's favorite pastimes was attending auction sales. He was notorious to only buy items when they were supercheap! He'd buy boxes of what looked like junk, but he'd have found some treasure in the box before they got to it. He'd buy and then resell at a profit! The auctioneers would always make jokes with him at these sales. If no one was bidding, they'd say, "Hey Carl, you need this, don't you?" Sometimes he'd buy it just to get the sale moving again. That was Carl. He was always trying to help out.

Pam loved to travel, and once they started going places, Carl enjoyed getting away also.

Their first family vacation was to visit his sister Judy in San Antonio, Texas, when Tara was two. Judy's husband, Chris, was showing them around, and driving in a big city was new to Tara. She said, "I better get my bell seat on—Chris is kind of crazy." They visited South Padre Island and saw white sand for the first time. Carl and Chris decided to grow moustaches on this trip. Carl only lasted two days—it just didn't look good—but Chris kept his for the next thirty-five years!

They went to Atlanta to visit Verla and saw a Braves' game; they went to Disney World several times and also took the kids to Hawaii. Family vacations were something special for all of them, and usually involved visiting family or friends. When Pam's sister Paula moved to Tennessee with her family, they went many times to visit them. It was always quality time and their children—cousins—remained connected.

Pam's employer, Dr. Wayne Skaloud, took the dental team on several trips for dental seminars. Carl loved going along and hanging out with the other husbands. On one occasion, the guys rented a convertible to drive around in Hawaii. Carl was driving when a bicycle cop motioned for him to come over to where he was. Carl pulled over and received a ticket because Steve King wasn't wearing a seat belt in the passenger seat. He never lived that one down. His nickname among this group was Courteous Carl. They said he was always thinking of others first, and he was. He always was.

On this same Hawaii trip, Pam and Carl got to take the convertible to a little village. They were having a great time exploring this little quaint area and they came up behind an older couple who were shuffling along. They both commented how grateful they were for taking the risk and paying for Carl to come with on this trip. Living life to the fullest means to never regret.

Life with Carl continued to be an adventure. Raising a family, taking vacations, working hard, and making time for fun made up this beautiful life.

Carl was involved in all of the kids' activities. Of course both Tara and Tyler were members of 4H—it was a family tradition. Carl helped them with their projects and like his dad, let them do it their way. They always loved choosing their pig and taking care of it to prepare for the fair. One year Tara's hog had diarrhea at the fair. Carl handed her a roll of toilet paper and told her it would be all right. She wiped its rear with toilet paper all the way to the show ring. He was right—it turned out fine and Tara learned perseverance.

Tara and Tyler also inherited love for baseball. Carl loved coaching their Little League teams. Tara's team lacked much talent, but Carl had very high expectations. It turned out, however, that fun was just as important as a winning season. Tyler practiced in the yard and became quite a good pitcher. He started sporting an attitude at one of his games. Carl pulled him from the game and let him sit on the bench. At the end of the game, Tyler apologized. Coaching and parenting aren't always easy but Carl was firm and consistent.

Because of Carl's history with St. Jude's, Pam felt called to organize St. Jude bike-a-thons. Tara and Tyler would ride their bikes along with other Galva youth around Wiley Park. The kids would get donations for each lap they made around the park. They usually collected around $2,000–$3,000 every year. Carl was so proud of them and happy to give back to St. Jude's!

After Carl's dad, Ed, had retired from farming, he was looking for a partner, and his cousin, Dan Bates, was doing the same. They were a perfect match. Dan was like another brother to Carl. They could talk for hours about their farming operation. He'd head over to Dan's every morning to plan out their day. They trusted God to water and provide sunshine for the crops to grow. They worked hard doing all that they needed to in order to get a good harvest.

One of the blessings of being his own boss, Carl was able to take Tara and Tyler to school every morning, and according to Carl, a Casey's donut was the best way to start their day.

Whenever Tara wanted to have cough drops or mints during class, he would always sign a note saying she could have them. Eventually Tara perfected his signature, and she would sign any papers they needed for school. He always trusted her.

Gift buying was normally Pam's job, but every year at Christmas Carl would go to Hathaway's, the local hardware store, to buy a toy for each of the kids. Pam liked to buy clothes and those weren't good gifts, in his opinion. Tyler always got some kind of ball—basketball, football, baseball . . . He wasn't so sure what Tara would like until the year he bought her a My Little Pony. She LOVED it! What was funny was that he continued that trend every year beyond the age she really liked them anymore. It became a family joke, and years later he found a box of them at an auction and he bought it for her!

When Tyler was about ten years old, he was outside playing with his basketball when he noticed the gate was open and a pig had gotten out. He got his dad to help him and they started chasing the pig toward the gate. That's when Tyler noticed a man was watching him from inside the barn. During this time there was a news story of a wanted man that was on the loose. They called him the Railroad Killer and he was known to be in Illinois. He had killed twenty-three people but they couldn't find him. The railroad tracks were only about a mile north of the farm. Tyler pointed out the man to Carl and they both slowly walked to the house. The man realized he had been seen and took off across the cornfield. Carl called the police and stood guard on the porch until the police arrived. I was right there with them. The police found the man on the other side of the field. They searched his bag and they did not find a weapon, so they sent him on his way.

Carl was always a calm presence in the storms of life; for example, the time Tara and Tyler were chasing each other through the house. Tyler slammed a door as Tara was reaching for him and her hand went through the glass, cutting her wrist. Blood was everywhere. Pam was frantically trying to find the phone number for the ambulance (it was before 9-1-1). The number was posted next to the phone, but Pam was too panicked to remember that. Carl said firmly, "Pam, just take her to the ER; I'll stay here with Tyler." That snapped her out of her frenzy, and she loaded Tara into the car and took off.

The doctor on duty, unfortunately, did not address the severed artery inside but just stitched up the cut on the outside. They came home and were settling in when Tara came back downstairs from her bedroom and said, "Mom, I forgot to take the Tylenol the doctor told me to take." That trip downstairs was Tara's guardian angel, Gabriel, saving her life! She had bled through the splint on her arm; they knew that wasn't normal and they went back to the ER. The same doctor on duty just bandaged it tighter. Sam was urging Pam not to leave, and so was one of the nurses by her frantic looks, but the doctor insisted it was fine and they went home.

All was OK until Tara sneezed about five days later and was immediately screaming in pain. They were shopping out of town so Pam took her to the ER in that town. Their response was: "I don't know what's going on inside but it looks OK outside." They sent them on their way.

Tara was crying and trying to be brave but she was miserable. Pam would call the first hospital and tell them she was in a lot of pain, but they were making her wait for the doctor who had treated her initially. He was finally on duty two days later and off they went. It's unfortunate that sometimes doctor egos can make their bedside manner less than perfect. This doctor knew they had visited another hospital and was obviously mad. Tara was ten years old, had been in pain for two days, was scared, and the doctor said to her, "I don't see anything wrong—you want me to cut it open?" Pam just kept praying. He did cut it, and blood went everywhere! Pam was holding Tara's face so she couldn't see. She pulled a chair over with her foot as she was feeling like she might pass out. She saw the panic in the doctor's face as he bandaged it up and ran to the phone. He arranged a vascular surgeon in another hospital to be ready when they got there by ambulance. Now he realized the artery had been severed. Apparently when he had bandaged it tighter, the ends had coagulated until the sneeze. Poor Tara had been bleeding internally, which was why she was so miserable. They rushed her to another hospital where it took three hours to reattach the severed artery by a vascular surgeon. The surgeon explained that the artery had gone up into her arm and they had to find it to reattach. Pam and Carl just sat in silence holding hands through that surgery. Sam, Gabriel, and I were there watching and praying.

Through it all, Carl never worried about what could've been or if surgery would be successful. Carl knew that God listened to prayers and answered them. He was always okay with whatever was God's will. Oh, how God enjoys those that trust Him.

Children are a gift given by God and sometimes parents make their children into their idols, like the golden calf in Moses's time. Parents are called to love and nourish and teach their children, but ultimately their job is to prepare them to know, love, and serve God. This is just their temporary home.

Family trip to Hawaii

Tyler farming with daddy

Tara and dad with her first car

CHAPTER 10

Carrying His Cross

*Then he said to all, "If anyone wishes to
come after me, he must deny himself and
take up his cross daily and follow me."*
—Jesus (Luke 9:23)

In 1993, Carl discovered that he had a hole in the bottom of his foot, from a nail that poked through the bottom of his tennis shoe—Carl and his tennis shoes! Because of his cancer treatments and spinal surgery as a child, he had very little feeling in his legs or feet. It was a progressive symptom that wasn't discovered until this happened. It took me forever to make him check his foot and it was pretty infected by the time he did. Turned out, the infection was in the bone. He went to the doctor and after two surgeries they started treating the infection with IV antibiotics. Because it was time to harvest, he convinced the doctors to let him do the IV treatments at home so he could go out to the field in between treatments.

Pam was very concerned about the risk of getting air in the line, as they warned them of the seriousness of an air embolism. Carl thought it was quite funny to cough, choke, close his eyes, and slump over while they were doing the treatment. Pam was not amused, but that was Carl!

It was a tough battle. The hole was in a place that was hard to heal, especially when Carl didn't want to sit at home with his foot propped up. He had multiple debridement procedures in Peoria and Galesburg, which kept him on crutches for months at a time. Life was complicated and frustrating but their new normal. Carl tried to keep life as usual for Pam and the kids. Tara was eleven years old and Tyler was seven years old. He never wanted to be a burden. When they were invited to a wedding, they got a room at the hotel so he could go and do his IV treatment and not miss the special event. After a full year of that it finally healed.

A few months later, Carl was out working in the field and he dropped a hog house on this same foot. His foot became swollen and purple. I was trying to convey the message that this was not normal. Pam would call the doctor's office and the girl who answered the phone would say if there is no pain then it's fine. This went on for six weeks; then, finally I convinced a nurse friend to tell them to insist on being seen.

The x-ray showed that he had broken all of the metatarsal bones in his foot and he had been walking on them, so now they were healing in a mass of bone. This made it impossible not to break down when he'd walk.

At this point, they knew they needed another opinion and went to Mayo Clinic in Rochester, Minnesota.

The foot would heal when he stayed off of it but after a time of walking, it would break down again. There were many trips to Minnesota. This turned out to be a bonding experience for Pam and Carl to have this uninterrupted time to talk. God's plan always involves communication. They would bring the kids with when they wouldn't miss school. Pam got reservations at a hotel with a pool, thinking that would be fun for the kids. But when she thought about all of the sick people at Mayo Clinic she couldn't let them swim. I was just glad they had some quality family time even in the midst of these struggles.

On one trip home from Mayo Clinic, the weather was progressively getting worse. Pam was driving as Carl was supposed to elevate his leg in the backseat. I knew there was a tornado in the area and got them to stop on the side of the road. Pam was praying the Hail Mary prayer out loud until the tornado passed over them.

There was another time in an ice storm when Carl drove the five-and-a-half-hour trip to avoid the added expense of a hotel room. He and Pam counted 223 cars in the ditches and prayed the whole trip! They couldn't remember the guardian angel prayer: "Angel of God, my guardian dear, to whom God's love commits me here, ever this day be at my side to light, to guard, to rule, to guide." But Sam and I were there protecting and guiding them all the same!

I was getting inside information from God Almighty regarding Carl's hog farming. So it became my mission to remind the doctor of the risk of infection involved with the hog operation. Finally the doctor insisted that Carl should get out of hog farming. He had a farm sale just a month before hog prices plummeted. Had he not gotten out, the sale would have been a bust. Another blessing and God-incidence they were grateful for.

Finances were a struggle, but God always provided. When things looked grim, Carl would put a piece of equipment he could do without on the front lawn with a For Sale sign on it. Someone always needed whatever it was they were selling, and they'd get just what they needed to pay the bills. They would also receive anonymous checks from people that knew they were in need.

One day a motorcycle gang out of Chicago stopped at the farm. They wanted to buy a piglet to raise and roast. Carl obliged and they drove off on their motorcycles with their piglet, some feed, and Carl had $200 in his pocket. These were all miracles God had orchestrated.

The doctors at Mayo Clinic were doing all they could. They tried boots, casts, crutches, and multiple debridement surgeries. Carl was one of the first patients to use a wound vac and that worked. The wound healed until he put pressure on it again by walking.

Carl was wearing one of his famous "boots" when he decided to join the dental team on a trip to Florida. The guys were out and about while the girls were in their dental meeting. They all got on the escalator and Carl's boot got caught. At first, he didn't want to make a big deal as he tried to pull it out, but that wasn't working. I got the attention of the others and they all frantically worked to get it unstuck before they got to the top. They got it out just in time! As I said, Carl had a life full of adventure.

In 2004, after all the attempts to get his foot healed permanently, it was the failed skin graft that was the deciding factor. It was time to do an amputation. At this point they were referred to a prosthetist, Ken. Another nearby farmer, Tom Nelson, had been involved in a farm accident and had lost his leg, and he had been a longtime patient of Ken's. That referral proved to be a new friendship and a bond, as Ken was also an amputee and understood this new challenge. He referred them to the surgeon, Dr. Pamela Davis. From experience, Ken knew she had the fewest problems with the healing process and fitting the prosthesis.

He set up the follow-up appointment to do some training on how to walk with this new leg. Carl just took off. Ken said he'd never had a patient who could walk that well the first time. This was Carl's third time he had to learn to walk. "I have the strength for everything through Him who empowers me." (Philippians 4:13)

The challenge then became watching for sores that would develop on the stump, and reacting before they became infected. Keeping Carl down was my biggest challenge. He knew he needed to let the sore heal before wearing the leg again. It just wasn't his nature to stop working. There were trips to the wound care center and infectious disease doctors even after the amputation.

As the leg changes shape continually there were new legs made every one to two years. The family joked they were going to market the discarded legs as lamps like on the movie *Christmas Story.*

As Carl was trying to keep life normal, he agreed to go on a family vacation with Paula's family to Myrtle Beach, South Carolina. Tara was doing a clinical there for her Physical Therapy doctorate. They made a lot of fun memories, but also had another miracle. Carl had been battling yet another wound, so some of the family went to visit the St. Benedict Abbey adoration chapel to ask for healing of Carl's leg. The next day it was completely healed. "Ask and you shall receive!" The problem is, sometimes people don't ask. Sometimes the answer is no or not yet, but you don't know unless you ask. God knows what is best for us; trusting in that is the key to a joy-filled life.

Shortly after this trip is when Tara's long-term boyfriend, Ben, asked Carl for his approval to ask Tara to marry him. Ben had become part of the family from an early age. They started talking in junior high and dated all through high school and college. Carl, in his matter-of-fact way, responded, "That would be fine." The planning began and this new chapter was exciting. Tara was graduating from St. Ambrose University with her doctorate in Physical Therapy in December, and the wedding was set for March 11, 2006.

A few years later, I made sure Pam noticed that Carl's right leg looked like it was bowing out when he walked. Carl didn't recall hurting it, but after much coercing they went to an orthopedic surgeon to have x-rays. A new cross to bear: the right knee was broken; he had a torn ACL, torn meniscus, and no good muscle to hold a knee replacement. Having just one good leg, over time, wore it down. He was always a puzzle for the doctors! The only thing they could suggest at this point was a metal brace to stabilize so the leg didn't give out. Even this didn't stop him from his attitude to just keep going.

The surgeon said he was inspired by Carl—he had patients with fewer problems than Carl who wanted disability. While disability is absolutely necessary for some, it just wasn't in Carl's plan. Carl continued to farm and work his electrical business, despite his obstacles. Scripture tells us, "Do everything without grumbling or disputing, that you may be blameless . . . shine as lights in the world." (Philippians 3:14, 15)[1] Also, "For the just man falls seven times and rises again, but the wicked stumble to ruin." (Proverbs 24:16)

The next step would have to be an above-the-knee amputation. He was not ready for that and due to the lack of pain, he could always keep going. The only thing was he wasn't able to attend many events if there was a lot of walking involved. He never complained and insisted everyone else go without him.

Through the twenty-two years of medical appointments, crutches, boots, and the amputation, Carl's unfailing hope inspired many. That's the thing about faith—for the Christian the situation is never hopeless.

Carl never gave up. For example, when the doctors told him to get out of hog farming and the crops weren't very profitable for a couple of years, he started working for a local electrician. Carl learned a lot from him. Dave DeMay—his cousin's husband—also started working there. They had some

---

1   English Standard Version Bible

good times. They were always joking around and it made the day fun. When business slowed down they were laid off, but when one door closes another opens.

Carl decided to do some electrical jobs on his own during the off-seasons. He did that for a few years with Dan's help, and then his son-in-law, Ben, Tara, and their family were going to move back to Illinois. Ben was interested in helping Carl both on the farm and with the electrical business. The timing was perfect just as God's plan always is.

Their new official business, Bates Electric, LLC, began by buying a bucket truck. Ben had been working for an electrician but Carl loved teaching him the business. Carl never wavered from having fun at work and playing pranks. I'll never forget the time he had Ben put up an electrical box: when he would leave, Carl would move it and then make him do it again, as it was in the wrong place. This happened three times, and Carl just kept telling him he was crazy and wouldn't admit he was messing with him. It was years later he confessed to playing that joke on him.

On the farm, he and Ben were a great team. Ben could help do some of the work it was hard for Carl to do, like filling the planter or changing the combine head from the corn head to the bean head. One day they were working on a piece of equipment to bend it. When it finally got bent the way Carl wanted, he turned around to Ben and said "Ta-Da!" What he didn't realize, even though I tried to warn him, was that he had stirred up a hornet's nest behind him and they both had to run. The prosthetic leg wasn't much for running so he got stung a few times. Ben could hear him trailing him saying *ouch, ooh, aaah* as he tried to run.

Carl also taught Ben how resourceful he could be. Carl asked him if he'd ever cut carbon fiber. Then Carl had him cut down his prosthetic leg so he didn't have to take it back to the prosthetist. He swore Ben to secrecy. That was another one of Carl's talents. He could find a way to make something work. It didn't always look pretty but it worked! God and I got a kick out of some of his "inventions" or "fixes"!

In the midst of carrying his cross, God intervened with an opportunity to help Carl see and feel God's love through his trials. The next chapter is about that experience.

Florida dental trip

Father-Daughter dance

Tyler's graduation from St. Ambrose University

CHAPTER 11

Cursillo (Kur-see-yo) - Short course in Christianity

Motto: Make a friend, Be a friend, Bring a friend to Christ

As guardian angels we love when our assignees agree to a "retreat" that will bring them closer to the Lord. There are many nondenominational weekends and other programs through different churches. Carl's brother-in-law and sister-in-law, Lou and Paula, had been through a movement called Cursillo. This program is put on by the Catholic Church. In the Diocese of Peoria it is open to everyone, regardless of their faith background. No distractions, no work, no responsibilities; just a time to be still. It helps each person in their own way to take a look at who they are, how Jesus fits into their lives, and how much He loves them. It also helps them to know ways in which they could love Him back, ways the Holy Spirit would help them discover.

Pam and Paula had both asked Carl and Lou to go to Cursillo many times. The program suggests that the men go through it first, and then the wives. The reason for this is that the men are harder to convince to go. The program hopes that married couples can share this experience.

It actually was six years before Lou finally agreed to go. He went in 1996. The impact it had on him was overwhelming, and when he told his story of what the weekend meant to him, Carl said, "Where do I sign up?" I did a little backflip for joy, as I knew Carl would gain a lot from this experience. He would especially feel God's love in a more profound way than ever before.

We guardian angels do our very best to share God's love, but at a retreat we have their undivided attention for three whole days—it is a powerful encounter. Carl went with his cousin Roger and Pam's dad, John. They all had a wonderful weekend; it was cleansing, eye opening, and life changing.

Carl was able to speak with a priest about that nagging fear that he would have every once in a while. The priest told him that it is not for us to know the future, or think about the past, but to live in the present.

Pam, her mom, and sister Leigh attended their Cursillo weekend the next month. Pam was feeling so blessed to have had this experience to share with Carl, as they both renewed their faith and trust in God's plan for their lives.

After these weekends, Carl, Lou, and Pam's mom went through RCIA and joined the Catholic Church. They all began a journey of faith that was new and fresh. Their faith was more central to their lives on a daily basis, not just a Sunday obligation. The Eucharist was what brought them in, the ability to nourish their souls with the body and blood of Christ. Jesus gave us this gift of Himself and it is the best gift ever.

"I am the living bread that came down from Heaven; whoever eats this bread will live forever; and the bread that I will give is my flesh for the life of the world."
(John 6:51)

As a new member of the parish, Carl got involved and became an officer for St. John's Catholic Church Knights of Columbus organization. They would hold a basketball shooting contest every year, an event that was fun for the kids. This organization supported local special needs charities and seminarians. At the annual pancake breakfast fundraiser in February you could find Carl, his brother-in-law, Lou Patty, and Jim VanDeVelde in the garage cooking up the sausage.

Prior to Cursillo, the one thing that Pam and Carl would fight about was Carl's drinking. He didn't drink often but when he did he sometimes would get pretty drunk. That was another thing that changed; he saw that his responsibility to his wife and his family was more important than a good time with the guys. The weekend revealed to him his purpose and he was reminded of what a blessing he was given in his wife and his children.

"Husbands, love your wives, even as Christ loved the church and handed himself over for her." (Ephesians 5:25) "That is why a man leaves his father and mother and clings to his wife, and the two of them become one body." (Genesis 2:24)

Carl didn't wear his faith on his sleeve, he didn't talk to people about Jesus, but he lived his faith and he treated everyone with the utmost respect. He definitely loved his neighbor.

This was a movement that they stayed involved in also. At one of the events Pam attended, she was given another message from Sam, her guardian angel, that God wanted her to hear. Over and over she heard, "Tell Carl you love him." Even though it scared her as to why she was getting this message, she told him about the message and told him she loved him as soon as she got home. Carl responded, "I love you more." It's not uncommon that in a marriage you can take your spouse for granted. This was another turning point in their marriage. A marriage God blessed again and again.

CHAPTER 12

Papa

"Best. Papa. Ever."

—Ava, Griffin, Grady DeWolfe

Carl was blessed to be a daddy, but being Papa was his over the top!

Ava was Carl and Pam's first granddaughter. Another God-incidence happened. Pam, Paula, Cheryl, and Brynn decided last minute to make a surprise trip to Knoxville, Tennessee. This is where Tara had taken her first physical therapist position at East Tennessee Children's Hospital. She wasn't due for two more weeks but it was a long Memorial Day weekend and they decided to make the trip. They got there late Friday night and Tara was surprised. They had a great weekend visit and then Sunday night Tara began to have contractions. The plan was that Pam and Carl would come as soon as she went into labor, but it was a question as to whether they'd get there for the birth, as it was a ten-hour drive. Well, Ava Kristine was born at 6:00 a.m. Monday, May 28, 2007. What a joy for them all to be there. Pam rode back with Paula, Cheryl, and Brynn and then picked up Carl and they drove back to Tennessee. This is when Tara and Ben decided to move closer to home, so Ava would have more Grandma/Grandpa time. Sixteen months later, on October 4, 2008, came their first grandson, Griffin Carl, and he looked just like Papa!

When they were tiny, Carl was a little leery of holding them too much, as they seemed so fragile. But the toddler age was prime Papa time. The kids loved him to pieces. Even though he couldn't run, play, or carry them, they absolutely adored him.

He called Ava "Skippy" because she was always bouncing around the house. And Griffin, his first grandson, he called George or Ralph just to be funny. He'd say, "What's the matter, Willis?" or ask them, "Where is the sky?" and when they would lift their arm to point up, he'd tickle them.

Griffin wanted to be with Papa as much as possible—they were connected, those two. He would ride in the combine for hours with Papa Carl; it was his favorite time of year. Griffin had a John Deere–themed birthday party where Papa gave combine rides in the field to all of his friends! Griffin wrote a story for school about his time with Papa:

I love going to pick and plant corn. I would ride in the combine and for my 7th birthday he gave me and my friends combine rides. It was really fun. When he came to check on the corn at my house I would ask if I could go to his house with him. I loved spending time with him. My favorite time was to pick corn at the Amazing Harvest. Me and my grandpa loved the Cubs. I wish he was there when the Cubs won the World Series. Me and him would watch the Cubs and drink Pepsi—it was the best. I have a lot of good memories with him over the years. I have not been picking corn in the last 2 years but this will be the last time for me on Papa's farm. He told me a lot of stories. When he was a kid he and his cousins told the girls there was quicksand at his grandpa's farm. I love him so much and so many memories. The end.

By Griffin DeWolfe

Ava also had an assignment at school to write about a special memory and she chose to write about the Amazing Harvest. Here is her report:

The Amazing Harvest for Grandpa Carl
by Ava DeWolfe

My grandma and aunts came over to my house and me, my mom, my grandma and my aunts made the food. Then we set out the food on a table in my front yard. Next the combines and tractors came and got lined up in their spots. There were

10 combines to get lined up. There was 1 tractor behind each combine. Next Grandpa Carl comes and we all say Hi. Then everyone gets in their combines and tractors and we pick all the corn at my house. I rode in the tractor with my dad and Griffin. Then we have lunch but the farmers didn't want to stop so they took their food in the combines and tractors and ate it in there. Then they went to Page street to pick the corn there. Then we all went to Wilsey's Farm and they picked the corn there and then we all ate dinner and I took pictures after dinner. Then me, my dad and some of the farmers rode in the back of the trucks and we went home. The farmers rode back to Wilsey's and finished picking the corn there. Then they went home and went to bed. That day we harvested 450 acres and it would have taken us two weeks but with the help of caring farmers we were able to get it done in 1 day.

Ava's and Griffin's hearts were broken and they will never forget what a wonderful Papa Carl they had. Oh what a wonderful reunion that will be someday! I'm telling you, it's the best thing ever.

Grady, grandchild number three, was always full of joy! You could see Carl light up when this little one was around.

If Carl couldn't be out farming or working, you could find him fixing the kids a snack. They were such loving kids who just took his one leg in stride. He would slip off his leg while just sitting on the couch and they would snuggle up to watch cartoons or one of his favorite westerns. Just spending time together was all they needed. Carl never took one moment for granted. Whatever his future held, this was precious time.

Carl, Ava, Griffin and Grady

CHAPTER 13

Decision

"The measure of a life, after all, is not its duration,
but its donation."
—Corrie ten Boom

Carl and I were faced with another challenge. God trusted me to guide Carl through it. With his gift of free will it was completely his decision. We just loved him and gave him strength. There had been hints along the way, but in the spring of 2015 Carl was asking Pam for some ibuprofen before bed quite frequently. This was a red flag for Pam because Carl rarely took any type of pain medication. When she asked Carl what was bothering him, he said his back hurt. He was sure it was just from bouncing around in the tractor. Of course, Pam and I knew that his back had not hurt the other forty years he had bounced around in the tractor. She asked the local physician assistant if he would check him out.

The physician assistant ordered some blood tests and an MRI and referred Carl to a neurosurgeon for the results. He also referred him to an infectious disease doctor to address another sore on his stump that wasn't healing. This resulted in a debridement and follow-up visits.

The neurosurgeon called Carl in to his office and said, "Well, I just had you come in to tell you that you don't need major back surgery." He did not have any answers to the reason for the pain. Carl asked, "You don't see a tumor?" Carl knew the pain cancer causes, and though he was not complaining, he was suffering pain he had suffered before.

For forty-four years, I knew Carl had the fear of his cancer returning. Other than when he spoke with the priest at Cursillo, he never mentioned it.

The neurosurgeon explained that the non-contrast MRI would not show tumors, so if it would make him feel better they could schedule one with contrast with his nurse. It was planting time, so Carl took ibuprofen and some muscle relaxers while he got through the planting season and finished changing out all the lights at St. John's for Bates Electric. He found that he couldn't eat more than a few bites and he felt full. He was losing weight and getting more and more uncomfortable.

Sam encouraged Pam to call the local physician assistant again. He scheduled a CT scan. On July 31, 2015, Pam and Carl were asked to come to his office. He told them that it was cancer, and it was very bad so it would be a fight! When you live in a small town and everyone knows everyone, this type of news is heartbreaking to give. The physician assistant had tears in his eyes as he gave them the news. Carl was quiet after this diagnosis and Pam asked him if he was mad at God.

He immediately looked at her and said, "No, He's given me miracles all my life. It's OK . . . I can't be greedy."

Cancer is never an easy diagnosis to hear, especially twice in your life. It was frightening, frustrating, and complicated to say the least.

An appointment was set up with an oncologist, radiologist, and urologist due to some kidney problems they also discovered. Pam, Carl, Tara, and Tyler all went to this appointment. In asking questions, the physicians learned about Carl's childhood cancer and decided it was all scar tissue and told him to return in three months to check his kidney function. *No cancer?* Tara questioned them with the diagnosis and how could they say this now. They decided then to get additional tests and so while they were hopeful this was true—it was not.

They then met with an oncologist who went over the options for treatment, but Carl had already made his decision. I knew that through his prayer to God: he had come to the realization that he wanted to enjoy every minute he had left.

The prognosis was six months with treatment, three months without. He had been through chemotherapy before and quality of life was more important to him. When he told this oncologist his decision, his response was: "It's the right decision; it's not going to go away."

To say people didn't understand his decision would be an understatement. Some were mad—why wouldn't he fight, why was he giving up. Carl wasn't surrendering to cancer, Carl was surrendering to Jesus. He felt he had lived an abundant life full of blessings. He did not fall for the lie of desperation to get a few more months filled with treatments and weakness. He heard Jesus calling and that's where he wanted to go.

Shortly before his death Carl had his last tractor ride. His brother-in-law Lou had offered to mow and got the old blue Ford tractor stuck over a stump. Lou was afraid to force it and possibly damage the tractor. Carl asked Tara to drive him out to take a look. At this point Carl was using a walker most of the time to get around. He asked Tara to get as close as possible to the tractor, so there were only two steps to get up into the tractor. Then he asked for a boost. Tara was eight months pregnant but was able to boost him up. He fired up the tractor and away he went! Over the stump like it was no big deal. Tara and her son watched in amazement. That was a good workday for Carl driving a tractor; shedding light in the darkness, and surprising people along the way.

As they shared the news with family, Carl continued to be his strong courageous self.

There were gatherings involving both sides of the family. Letters were written and shared with him about how he had touched their lives. All of his nieces and nephews came to visit—sometimes it was a party in the bedroom, but he always enjoyed the company. He didn't show emotion until he heard how upset the grandkids were when they heard that Papa was going to die.

Leigh's guardian angel guided her to draw nearer to God. She went back to college and began working for the Catholic Church. Carl's mom called her Reverend Leigh. She had some serious talks with Carl about his faith—God spoke to him through her.

Grady was only eighteen months old when Papa Carl went to be with Jesus, but Grady remembers him. They would play blocks and toys on the bed in Carl's last weeks. Carl would put on a smile and enjoy these moments. Ava and Griffin were also spending quality time with him.

Friends came to visit too. Bill from Florida, Dan from Arizona, and many local friends and cousins. They were all such a blessing in those last days. It is a hard thing for people to visit someone who is sick, and especially when that person is dying. It is a corporal work of mercy that God gives those willing to step out of their comfort zone the strength to perform. They are remembered in Heaven by the people they visited.

At the end of his life, Pam asked if he had any regrets . . . he said, "Only that I didn't go see where Dan lived." Another of Tara's clinical visits was in Scottsdale, Arizona. Pam arranged with her cousin, Erika, for Tara to stay with her in Mesa, Arizona. Pam drove Tara to Arizona and then flew home so Tara could have a car to commute. She tried to get Carl to go with them and he could've visited his high school friend, Dan Brooks, who lived in nearby Chandler. Carl thought it was too expensive and didn't go. This was the trip he regretted not taking. I wish he would've gone, but what a blessing to only have one regret.

There were other precious moments during this time of reflection and serious conversations. Carl told Pam, "This is not how it was supposed to be . . . we were supposed to grow old together." He also made sure she knew he loved her and told her, "I've always loved you." God's love is just like that—forever and unconditional.

Pam asked him to give her baby sister, Jennifer, a hug and he said, "Oh yeah—I will." She also gave him some special intentions to pray for once he was in the presence of God in Heaven, and he agreed.

When Carl was having a particularly bad day, he asked Pam to call the kids over. He wanted to make sure they knew he loved them and had always been grateful for the miracles they were for him. He also wanted to know if there was anything he could give them to remember him by. They didn't want anything he hadn't already given them—the best dad they could have ever asked for. He told them both how very proud of them he was.

Carl told the family to do what was best for them and not to keep farming if it didn't make sense. He did give Pam a timeline of how things run on the farm—after all, that was always his job. He wanted to do something for the grandkids and mentioned a playhouse. Within days, some friends built one and he was able to check it out.

"Consider it all joy, my brothers, when you encounter various trials, for you know that the testing of your faith produces perseverance. And let perseverance be perfect, so that you may be perfect and complete, lacking in nothing."
(James 1:2-4)

One of the last times a group of their friends all got together was in September of 2015. They met at Pam and Carl's home to plant a tree in honor of their thirty-fourth wedding anniversary. Pam's work family at Galva Family Dentistry supported her through Carl's illness. One of Pam's closest coworkers, Christy, gave Carl a card and said she was changing his nickname from Courteous Carl to Courageous Carl. She told him she respected his decision and admired his confident peace that only comes from God. She said she knew his previous trials and fight were always for his family and his love for them.

People underestimate the power of encouraging words. Carl was touched by these words.

One of Pam's employers, Dr. Scott Bialobreski, had experienced this horrible disease when his mom had succumbed to glioblastoma multiform in his second year of dental school. His dad had been given as much time off as he needed. Galva Family Dentistry paid that forward for Pam. The work family brought meals to their home and also to the hospice home in the end days. Their corporal works of mercy were abundant throughout the trials. "Not all of us can do great things, but we can do small things with great love." (St. Mother Teresa)

Their church friends were also bringing meals. Carl would rave about the food as there were some great cooks!

Two of his last visitors were Roger and Vicki Bates, who brought dinner over. This was right after the Cubs lost and were not going to be in the World Series. They were so close to making it. Carl said, "At least they beat the Cardinals!"

He was entered into a hospice program that would give Carl and the family a resource to help keep him comfortable and someone to ask questions. Rita was an amazing nurse who told the family exactly what to expect and how to handle the situation. Carl always wanted the truth. When he couldn't get his prosthetic leg on due to swelling but wanted to get out of bed, it was starting to affect his safety. This last night at home, Pam took Carl into the bathroom in the wheelchair—he told her she could go, he'd be fine. When he wasn't calling her, she went in—and he had transferred himself into the bathtub. He then confessed it probably wasn't the best idea but he had decided to take a shower. This took all of his energy but Pam was able to get him back into the wheelchair and back into bed.

This was the night he asked Pam to pray the Divine Mercy chaplet with him. This was a prayer Father Burns had prayed with him earlier that day and is a powerful prayer at the time of death. The fact that he asked to pray this prayer made Pam aware that he was preparing himself for his transition. She told him to follow along with the prayer card as she knew the prayers. Let me explain that normally this prayer is said over five decades like a rosary. Father Burns had only done one decade when he visited. So Pam was on the third decade and Carl said, "Isn't that a little overkill?" In his opinion, one would be enough, and I believe God would agree. He hears the prayers in our hearts.

This was also the night I wanted to make sure Pam knew how much Carl had loved her. They had some beautiful moments and he gave her his last real kiss. Pam found out later this was a specific prayer request from her coworker and prayer group—that she would have these special moments. God is good.

Pam then slept next to the bed on the floor to make sure he didn't try to get up in the night and get hurt. This is when the decision was made to move Carl to the Richard L. Owens Hospice Home, a beautiful and peaceful place to spend his last days. That first night they had put Pam's bed next to his and took the rail down so that she was able to touch him. She whispered to him all of the blessings they had experienced, professed her love for him, and even with some of the trials they had financially, she was grateful for his providing and always being there for her and their family. She really didn't know if he heard any of it but I know he did. All of his family was there, spending time together in the huge gathering rooms as they shared stories and memories. Ernie told a lot that no one had heard before! Laughter and tears were shared. Carl was able to tell each of them he loved them that first night before slipping into a coma.

A local organization called Moments by Mutti had donated hotel rooms and provided a group dinner for all of the family on those last few days. This organization was created by a family who lost their mom to cancer. They decided to help other families by creating special memories "moments" after a diagnosis is made.

Carl had four priests come to give him last right blessings—Father Eugene Radosovich, Father John Burns, Father Bulek, and Father Bruce Lopez. It was Fr. Bruce Lopez who gave the final blessing of extreme unction. Fr. Lopez had brought him into the Catholic Church and now he was sending him home to Heaven. The whole family was around the bed while he prayed this powerful prayer—everyone felt the Holy Spirit present. At the end of the prayer, Fr. Lopez got in Carl's face and said, "Carl, I know you can hear me, your family will be fine. It's time for you to go home—Don't be afraid!"

A few hours after this prayer, Carl went home on All Saints Day November 1, 2015.

In a state of grace, my job is to help them to Heaven, to have a peaceful death, ward off demons, and work as an advocate at this most intense hour of death. As I said before, Carl knew I was there at this most precious moment.

Of course, in pure Carl fashion, it was the end of daylight saving time at 2:00 a.m. on November 1, 2015. It took a minute or two to figure out what day it was because he died at 1:40 a.m.!

Carl and grandson, Grady

Anniversary tree planting party in September 2015 Front Row: Lou Patty, Middle Row: Carl, Randy Reiman, Ron Franklin, John Holt, Roger Bates, Denny Tarleton Back Row: Kim Reiman, Pam, Cari Nelson, Barb Franklin, Vicki Bates, Paula Patty, Janell Holt, Joyce Tarleton

CHAPTER 14

The Most Amazing Harvest

"I have competed well; I have finished the race;
I have kept the faith."
(2 Timothy 4:7)

The Most Amazing Harvest was the brainchild of Carl's cousin and partner in farming, Dan Bates. When Dan came to what they knew would be their last visit, it included a hug and "I love you."

Carl was overwhelmed and honored by the gesture of all his friends and colleagues. Even though he was not having a good day physically, he insisted on being there in the morning where a group picture was taken of all the farmers there to help. Carl also went out to thank all of them when they stopped for dinner. The farmers were spread out with their dinner plates on hayracks set up for this community meal of lasagna, salad, and garlic bread prepared by his family and friends. Carl sat in his big red truck on the side of the field and they all took turns coming over and talking to him. His voice was weak but he was so grateful. Each person there knew they had done a good thing for a good guy and he appreciated them very much.

Carl was a humble guy and hated to get his picture taken (in fact most snapshots of him include his hand in front of his face) but here was this story with his picture being spread around the world. Living in the Midwest, you see this type of giving and service to others as the norm. To people outside of the rural communities, they find this amazing.

Many people reacted to the story with likes and comments. Prayers were offered from all over, and these prayers held everyone together. Letters were sent to Carl—following are two of those letters, one from someone who knew him as a child and saw the story from Florida, and one from a stranger in Georgia who felt moved to reach out to him.

Dear Carl and family,

It's Wendy from White Eagle Camp. I loved and hated the story I see about you on the internet—holding you and yours very gently in our hearts and prayers, and hoping for miracles on the horizon. It was a great story, but nothing less than one would expect from the good people around you, no doubt inspired by the kind of person you always were.

We are too young for all this—one minute we are bouncing around on the Potawatomi Flats and the next we are all grown up with families of our own and writing in ink.

I see a beautiful wife on the internet and lovely children—maybe grandchildren?—and certainly a loving community. Please give my love to your sisters and your mom. As hard as this is for those who love you, the blessing of your childhood bout with this same hateful disease is that we all knew how precious you were early on, and how fortunate we were to have known you.

I'd recognize you anywhere. I remember your uncomplaining childhood, your natural optimism, the difficulty your family had of keeping you still as you charged through life, ready to take it all on with energy, optimism and gratitude. I also remember sweet Judy and adorable Verla, at a time in our lives when the rest of us were busy pounding on our siblings, caring for you tenderly. Your bravery as a child was remarkable but not anything you ever dwelt upon, or even mentioned as I recall. I think I had to pry the facts out of your sisters, but I would never have guessed.

We'll keep you and those who love you on our prayer list—I'm sorry you need it, but it's a good place to be. I pray for total healing, but also for you to feel the love you've spread around over your lifetime all coming back to you at once. The pictures on the internet would probably have made me cry even if I'd never known you. Before I read the story, just the headline made my heart sure you were the organizer of that miracle, and I guess that was actually correct. You were the karmic organizer.

Things have turned out well for me: twin boys, 18 now, and my daughter is 13, all precious, good kids. I've got a houseful of pets and a yard full of poultry—never really get the farm out of the girl, I guess. If you get to Heaven before I do (and you never know, really, do you?) please watch over them, too, and if I should beat you there, I'll return the favor. I'm sure it's a lot like White Eagle Camp. I'm glad your life has turned out so beautifully, and hope the journey is longer than we think, and gentle from here on out, and abundant blessings keep your heart full all your days.

Sending you love, Wendy

As Pam read this letter to him she was moved to tears. She asked Carl, "Doesn't this make you want to cry?" Carl answered, "Almost".

Dear Carl & Family –

You don't know me from Adam, but I wanted to send you a note and let you know that I am thinking about you, your family, neighbors, friends and am lifting you up in prayer! You see, I saw the story of your corn harvest on Facebook and it moved me to tears. Why? Because it is wonderful to see there are still good people in this country who practice the beliefs we were founded on. Love your neighbor as yourself. (Mark 12:31) What a testimony your community has made to the hundreds of thousands of people this story has reached! Way to go Galva!

Both my father in law and father have had cancer. I know where you are and I will lift you all up for strength and comfort. My husband, myself and our kids had to bail the hay fields for my father in law when he was sick. It was hard long hours, but nothing like your farming!

So I just wanted you to know God has laid you, your family and sweet friends on my heart. When he moves your spirit—I have to be obedient and respond. So I'm enclosing a little $ as my way to let you know you have neighbors even farther away that love and care about you!

I wish I had a combine and just lived down the street—we would've helped for sure! But since I'm not, maybe you can pay for fuel, groceries, medical bills or whatever you or your family might need.

Please give hugs to the Bates family for us. High fives to the neighbors for showing everyone how great Galva is, and our love to our brothers and sisters in Christ.

Blessings to you and yours, Emily

p.s. I'm not a stalker—just saw your Bates Electric shirt in the photo and looked up the address! Just in case you were wondering how I figured out an address.

The Most Amazing Harvest farmers

CHAPTER 15

The Most Amazing Funeral

*"A farmer can have no better crop than
a bountiful harvest of friends."*
—Kathy Mays

The funeral was planned. His only request for the funeral was no suit and tie—he was not a suit-and-tie kind of guy! They found a barn board casket that was perfect. A video was created with several songs that included "Why I Farm" by the Henningsens, Journey's "After All These Years," and "Flawless" by Mercy Me. These songs and the lyrics fit his life and were accompanied with lots of pictures. The calling hours were held at St. John's Catholic Church in Galva with over eight hundred people attending. It was mentioned that the number of people was a testament that Carl was a farmer of men just as Jesus' apostles were fishers of men.

The funeral was at St. John Paul II church in Kewanee, Illinois, where Tara had gotten married and the grandkids attended Visitation Catholic School. Deacon John, Pam's dad, gave the homily:

Today we are celebrating the life of Carl Bates. Carl was born on July 14, 1960, in Kewanee, the son of Edward and Carol (Mowers) Bates.

He married Pamela Holevoet on Sept. 19, 1981, in Galva. She survives as well as his mother, Carol, of Galva, a son, Tyler Bates, and a daughter, Tara (Ben) DeWolfe, both of Galva.

Three grandchildren: Ava, Griffin, and Grady, and an expected grandchild due in December.

His siblings: a sister, Judy (Chris) Simonson, of Janesville, WI; a brother, Ernie (Sarah) Bates of Lanark, Illinois; and sister Verla (Scott) Hemrick, of Johns Creek, GA, and many aunts, uncles, nieces, nephews, and cousins.

He was preceded in death by his father, Ed, and sister, Carrie, in infancy.

In earlier years he had been active in 4H and played softball. He was baptized Methodist as an infant. In 1997, Carl attended Cursillo #539 with me and his cousin. Carl then came into the Catholic Church on Easter 1998.

Carl was always positive in his attitude. He never looked down on anyone. He wanted to be your friend. They say that if a person can have 5 good friends at the end of their life, they have accomplished some greatness. Well, I have to say Carl made an impression on a lot of people.

As our first reading stated, God tried him and found him worthy of himself, as gold in the furnace, he proved him. And because grace and mercy are with his holy ones, his faithful shall abide with him in love.

Carl was not one who preached the gospel but he lived the gospel. So when we look at the second reading we may have to suffer through various trials. So that the genuineness of our faith, more precious than gold that is perishable, even though tested by fire, may prove to be for praise, glory and honor at the revelation of Jesus Christ.

We have to say that Carl had those trials in his early years, and then in the last 22 years after stepping on a nail, but I never heard him complain.

Then cancer came back with no hope. I remember Pam telling me she asked Carl if he was mad at God, and he said, No. 15 years ago I told him we were praying for God to heal his legs, and he said, "God has blessed me so much already. I am still here, and I was told I couldn't have kids and we have 2 of them. I have been blessed."

As we look back on the last 2 months on all the miracles we have to think about:

First, every Sunday, after Mass, I took Carl communion. When I did this I felt that Carl was very humble as I read the readings and we prayed the prayers. I felt Carl's heart was very open to what he was receiving and that was the Body of Christ.

God blessed us with all these wonderful friends and neighbors to harvest the crops for Carl. With all the publicity we had and all those people praying for Carl the family felt blessed and it gave them peace and strength.

When Carl was still conscious, as a family we all wrote notes and read them to him about how we felt about him and the memories we shared.

We were pretty much all in accordance with each other that Carl was a father in the image of God. He was not afraid to tell you if your attitude was not right, but always praised you for doing good in anything you tried to accomplish.

Then we hear today, "Amen, Amen I say to you, unless a grain of wheat falls to the ground and dies, it remains just a grain of wheat. But if it dies, it produces much fruit."

So, Lord God, you are the glory of believers and the life of the just. Your son redeemed us by dying and rising to life again. Our brother, Carl, was fruitful and believed in our own resurrection. Give to him the joy and blessings of the life to come.

Carl spent a lifetime in quiet, faithful care for his loved ones . . . And that's all of you.

May our God be blessed.

One of the journalists who were instrumental in the viral story of the Amazing Harvest also attended the funeral and wrote this article.

Sending off Mr. Carl Bates—The Most Amazing Funeral from The Most Amazing Harvest
by Joy Hernandez-Butler

I went to the funeral of a stranger today. I never knew Carl Bates in real life.

His funeral started with a family procession led from Galva by the Galva Fire Department and one of its engines. The funeral itself took place in Kewanee, at St. John Paul II church. Family members mentioned that they were worried the Galva church wouldn't be able to hold enough people. St. John Paul II was barely able to hold all of the people. I'm not exaggerating when I say there was maybe enough room for another 6 people and that was it.

Mr. Bates had a large family, and an especially large extended family. They filled many of the pews. He had a large farmer family- the people that came together to give him the most amazing harvest. They filled the pews as well. His father-in-law, a deacon, delivered the eulogy. Other family members helped deliver the service. Mr. Bates was laid to rest in a casket constructed of barn wood. It was an amazing service.

The funeral procession wound its way back out to Galva to the Galva Cemetery. The Galva Fire Department engine led the way, with in-town help from the Kewanee Police Department and the Galva Police Department.

Traffic dutifully stopped at intersections and waited patiently for the procession to roll by. What causes a Kewanee traffic jam? A healthy dose of respect.

Just before the Bates Farm, a farmer was working in his own field, his big green tractor pulling equipment along. He stopped his work out of reverence to the passing procession. I was told later that he was one of the participating farmers in the most amazing harvest. Harvest will continue, there is work to be done to make sure the fields are ready for next year. But he took a few minutes to remember his neighbor.

At the Bates Farm, the procession slowed. A family friend rolled out into the lead, driving Mr. Bates' red tractor. The sky was the perfect shade of blue. The clouds were little fluffy cotton balls. Looking out over the fields, as we rolled along, I knew why one of my friends in the area always refers to this as "God's Country." It seemed especially fitting today.

The Galva Cemetery is just outside of town, and just outside of the county, in Knox County. Our cars packed the cemetery roads, and we all gathered around his grave, with Mr. Bates' family under the tent. The wind was crisp and the graveside portion of the service was short. At the end, the priest said that we don't say good-bye to Carl, we say "see you later." Nearby fields had been harvested, and dried corn husks blew across the grass.

We all found our way back to Kewanee, to Visitation Catholic School, for refreshments and conversation. I got to meet quite a bit of the Bates family. There's a lot of them. I was told how camera-shy Carl was. How humble he was. What was all this fuss about? What do you mean people around the world know about this harvest? Those were the questions he asked, but family told me he enjoyed it, knowing that the world cared. Sometimes, the most humble are the most deserving of grand attention . . . but it will be like pulling teeth to get them to admit it.

Mr. Bates' widow remarked about how it was such a wonderful distraction, the viral attention to the harvest. It offered solace at a time when hearts were hurting. Something else to think about. Now it's a great worldwide scrap book: The story of farmers doing what they do-helping each other in a time of need-and the world paying attention, giving their thoughts or prayers to Carl, and recognizing kindness that is at the same time dutiful and worthy of recognition.

They told me of a family member with international ties, who, at a world event, was shown the story. The family member was known to be from the Midwest, from Illinois, did he know of this area? These people? He had to compose himself: he knew. They were his family and friends.

The pictures were seen around the world. The Bates family fielded calls not just from local journalists, but from well-wishers in Italy, even Sweden (which if you know the history of Galva, is about as full circle as you get). People that grew up in our area were standing up in their current communities, shouting, "I'm from there! That's my home!" Proud of the representation of their hometown.

I went to the funeral of a stranger today. I left feeling like I had a good grasp of who Carl Bates was. I told his family, if I had to infer, to assume, based on the actions of his family, his friends, his farmers, and his community, I'd say Carl was a pretty amazing fellow. And there'd be a deafening chorus that I was right. I've covered big funerals before-state legislators, fallen heroes-and today's funeral ranks right up there with those. Globally, the internet sent Carl off in style. Locally, his family and friends and community sent him off in the most amazing way.

There were a lot of thank-you's passed around today. But the biggest thank-you goes to Dan Bates, Carl's cousin, and the farmers that showed up on September 25th.

Without all those involved, we wouldn't have had so much to talk about these last six weeks. And we wouldn't have made a world of friends.

Prayer of St. Francis of Assisi

Lord make me an instrument of Your peace.
Where there is hatred, let me sow love;
Where there is injury, pardon;
Where there is doubt, faith;
Where there is despair, hope;
Where there is darkness, light;
And where there is sadness, joy.

O Divine Master, grant that I may not so much seek to be consoled as to console;
to be understood as to understand;
to be loved as to love;
for it is in giving that we receive;
it is in pardoning that we are pardoned;
and it is in dying that we are born to eternal life.

In Loving Memory of
Carl E. Bates
July 14, 1960 - November 1, 2015

Funeral Mass
Visitation Church,
St. John Paul II Parish
Kewanee, Illinois
Saturday, November 7, 2015
10:00 a.m.

Celebrant
Fr. John Burns

Homily
Deacon John Holevoet

Interment
Galva Cemetery
Galva, Illinois

Rux Funeral Home ~ Galva, Illinois

CONCLUSION

Messages from Heaven

"Blessed be the God and Father of our Lord Jesus Christ,
who in his great mercy gave us a new birth to a living
hope through the resurrection of Jesus Christ from the
dead, to an inheritance that is imperishable, undefiled,
and unfading, kept in Heaven for you, who by the power
of God are safeguarded through faith, to a salvation that
is ready to be revealed in the final time."

(1 Peter 1:3-5)

As mentioned earlier, the funeral video had the Mercy Me song "Flawless." This song played on the radio from the church to the cemetery. It has played at other times when it truly felt like a message from Heaven. This song also reminded Pam of the memory of Tyler at five years old seeing a man with only one leg. In his innocence he said, "Mom, when that man gets to Heaven he'll have both legs again." It was a moment that Sam never let her forget and what a blessing to know Carl was whole again in Heaven.

"No matter the bumps, no matter the bruises, no matter the scars, still the truth is the cross has made, the cross has made you flawless." (Mercy Me)

For months following the funeral, Grady would want to watch that funeral video over and over again. Whenever he would hear the song "Flawless" by Mercy Me, he would say "Papa's song." Mercy Me was having a concert nearby and they decided they would all go—even Grady. They realized Grady thought Papa was singing the song and this meant he would see Papa at the concert. They told him someone else would be singing it and he said, "Well do they know it good?"

Pam decided the following Easter was a good time to get away with her immediate family, and they all went to the beach in Florida. She had a dream the first night they were there. In the dream she had forgotten to let Carl know they had arrived in Florida safely. She called and he was over-the-top excited about this trip, asking if the kids were having a good time and telling her to enjoy this vacation. This was not his normal reaction in this world—he never really got over-the-top excited about anything! He probably would have thought it was too much money to spend also. Pam was comforted that he truly was happy and thriving in his new home.

I can't deny or confirm whether Carl had anything to do with it, but the Cubs WON the World Series the following year!

On the anniversary of The Most Amazing Harvest, Pam and Tara had gone out to eat. When they got to the restaurant they heard "Flawless" so they sat in the car to listen. When they went inside—Pam went into the restroom. On the floor were two kernels of field corn. Only God could arrange this crazy God-incidence that I'm sure was Carl's idea! Some people have seen feathers or pennies that remind them of their missing loved ones—Carl used corn.

The Galva Fire Department and their chief, Denny Tarleton, honored Carl's memory with a picture of the Harvest on Engine #13 for his service to the Fire District.

On the third anniversary of The Most Amazing Harvest, a mural was painted on one of the prominently seen buildings in Galva. A tribute to how this community comes together for one of their own. They were able to get most of the farmers together again for a picture in front of this mural.

In 2017 Tyler and Steve King's son, Aaron, decided to hold a golf tournament in honor of their dads. The proceeds are given to high school seniors pursuing a future in agriculture. They have also donated the extra to the Galva Fire Department. This has been a huge success and a testament to the integrity of these two men.

I hope and pray that reading this story has inspired you a little. All God's people have a story, including you. May you take a look back at your life and know that your guardian angel has been with you. He has been guiding, protecting, praying, and communicating God's love to you. Have you been listening? I hope so!

God bless you and keep you all the days of your life!

Yours truly,
Gus

Here are Carl and Pam's grandchildren, Grady and Cade waving at "Papa's firetruck" in the Fourth of July parade.

Eric Bates, Dan Bates, Warren Werkheiser (standing in for Ron Werkheiser), Pete VanDeVelde, Alex Stisser, Aaron King, Jim VanDeVelde, Jason Bates, Al Werkheiser, Lou Patty, Ava DeWolfe, Tara DeWolfe, Lydia DeWolfe, Grady DeWolfe, Ben DeWolfe, Paula Patty, Brynn Patty, Justin Bates, Pam Bates, Tyler Bates, Cade DeWolfe, Griffin DeWolfe, Mark Fargher, Carl Werkheiser, Bob Collister, Nick Johnson, Anthony Mertz, Craig Anderson, Randy Collister, Nathan Wallace, Mike Werkheiser, Keith Collister, Roger Wallace, Ernie Hulstrom, John VanDeVelde, Steve Bell, Wilbur Nelson, Greg Fargher, John Holevoet, Mike Rumbold

ABOUT THE AUTHORS

Pam Bates and Paula Patty are identical twins. They do most things together including working together at Galva Family Dentistry. Pam is Paula's boss, which is how it's always been—she is nine minutes older! Paula, however, was the experienced writer, having written a column called "Where Are They Now." She interviewed former residents who left this small town but never forgot their roots. This is their first book; it was a beautiful faith-strengthening experience as well as a healing process for Pam after the loss of her husband, Carl. They both live in Galva, Illinois, and love their small-town community.

CPSIA information can be obtained
at www.ICGtesting.com
Printed in the USA
JSHW031958130720
6612JS00017B/135